SOUTHERN COACHES IN

Compiled by Michael Welch in association with Ted Crawforth, Roger Merry-Price, Trevor Rapley and David Wigley.

© Noodle Books & Michael Welch 2010

ISBN 978-1-906419-45-5

First published in 2010 by Kevin Robertson under the **NOODLE BOOKS** imprint
PO Box 279, Corhampton, SOUTHAMPTON. SO32 3ZX

www.noodlebooks.co.uk

Printed in England by Ian Allan Printing Ltd.

Front cover - A trio of coaches awaiting disposal at Horsted Keynes on 27 September 1959: the walkway to Horsted Keynes signalbox is in the foreground. They are (from l to r.) SR composite corridor No.5596, LSWR third No.194 and SR brake third No.4061. No.5596 was ordered in 1928 for the Hastings line services and actually entered traffic in October 1929. This coach had extremely generous two-a-side seating in the first class while the third class compartments accommodated six passengers seated three-a-side. Note that the bodyside door stops just short of the bottom of the coach side panelling, the edge of the coach floor being visible. This is a characteristic of Hastings line Restriction '0' stock. The vehicle in the middle was constructed by the LSWR and entered service in November 1898 as third No.88. It was first withdrawn in March 1935, fitted with a new underframe which gave it a new lease of life and lasted in traffic until finally condemned July 1959. The carriage on the right of the shot is No.4061, a four compartment third brake built in mid-1928, reportedly by the Metropolitan Carriage, Wagon and Finance Company, and allocated to set No.447 for London to West-of-England services. It was taken out of service in July 1959.

Colour-Rail

Title page - The system on the Isle of Wight was operated entirely with vintage locomotives and coaching stock until the end of steam. This was, of course, a result of its physical isolation from the mainland. Set No.485 was photographed at Cowes on 25 June 1957 during the course of a gravity shunting manoeuvre while the locomotive ran-round. After the passengers had been detrained, the locomotive would be uncoupled and push the coaches back beyond the points. The engine would then proceed to the buffers, the points would be changed and it could then run-round while the coaches re-entered the station under gravity. One wonders if the operating authorities at Waterloo had approved this procedure - assuming they knew about it, of course. The formation of sets on the Island tended to be fairly fluid and on the occasion of this photograph, Set No.485 consisted of three SECR vehicles with one LBSCR coach furthest from the camera.

R. C. Riley

Back cover top - Next stop, the breaker's yard. A long line of withdrawn coaches at Gatwick Airport on 15 April 1960 awaits movement to a scrap yard at Newhaven. The vehicle nearest to the camera is former Royal train carriage No.7919 which was built by the SECR in 1905 and later converted to an invalid saloon. The coach is described elsewhere in this album.

Colour-Rail

Back cover bottom - A close-up view of restaurant first coach No.7677 taken at Bournemouth Central in the mid-1960s. These were really stylish and luxurious carriages for their time and were built in 1947/48 for use in the prestigious Bournemouth dining sets. The set number 290 is visible on the solebar. Note the antimacassars and table lamps.

Tim Robbins

INTRODUCTION

In the late-1950s, when photography of railway subjects in colour became much more commonplace, there was still an amazing hotchpotch of locomotive-hauled coaching stock in use on the Southern Region of British Railways. Ancient pre-grouping carriages could still be found on branch and secondary line services while coaches from the Maunsell and Bulleid eras were in widespread use on main line trains, including prestigious named expresses.

Among the strange specimens still to be found active was 'gate set' No.373 which had been originally built by the LSWR in June 1914 for use on branch line services. This was the last survivor of a small number of similar sets fitted with collapsible metal trellis gates rather than doors, hence they were universally known as 'gate sets'. Another interesting LSWR survivor was 'emigrant' set No.735, the coaches of which were built way back in 1907/08 to a composite loading gauge for use on trains conveying East European emigrants who were *en route* to America. This set lasted on the South Eastern Section until early 1961. The LBSCR 'Balloon' coaches were originally constructed for use on a pull-push basis on various branch lines plus routes where there were a large number of stations/halts in a short distance, such as Brighton to West Worthing. The nickname of these vehicles stemmed from the fact that they were built to the very generous LBSCR loading gauge and were therefore confined to former 'Brighton' lines after the 1923 grouping. None survived into the 1950s in passenger use, but one did last at the back of Lancing works until the early 1960s. A further fascinating 'Brighton' coach was No.S3847S, dating from December 1921 and had unusual open-sided compartments. This was allocated to a set until February 1952 when it became, in effect, a one coach 'set' for use on the Pulborough - Midhurst - Petersfield branch, one of Southern Region's most unremunerative backwaters where passengers could often be counted on the fingers of one hand. When this route closed in 1955, No. S3847S found little further employment, but it did make appearances on the re-opened 'Bluebell' line between Lewes and East Grinstead. The SECR was responsible for some of the weirdest designs particularly when it came to providing passengers access to a lavatory. Some of their composite lavatory vehicles possessed two toilet compartments, but only a minority of the passengers were able to obtain access to a lavatory as most were accommodated in closed compartments. Other noteworthy SECR designs included the 'Continental' stock with inward opening doors and the notorious ten-compartment third vehicles (two of which are preserved on the Bluebell Railway) which had the hardest seats imaginable. In the late-1950s, forty-six vintage pull-push sets still survived on the SR, although doubts over their crash worthiness and fears that they could catch fire in the event of a collision within the electrified area ensured their early demise, the last running in the Tunbridge Wells area in late 1962.

When the Grouping occurred in 1923, the Southern Railway naturally started to standardise to a degree and consequently Maunsell's designs appeared across the system. However, even then a wide range of coaching stock types was built, including the 'Nondescript' brake vehicles that boasted armchair luxury, and the restriction '0' stock built especially for use on the Hastings line where narrow tunnels prevented the use of coaches built to the standard width. Passengers may not always have appreciated the restricted width of this stock, as the first class compartments sat only two-a-side, with just three -a-side in third class. In 1933 a batch of thirty open saloon coaches was ordered and these had steel panels screwed on to the framework flush with the windows, and this feature gave a much less cluttered appearance than previous types. Coaches built to this design, which started to appear in 1935, were widely considered to be Maunsell's best design. Here again, an example, No.S1309S, is preserved on the Bluebell line.

After the end of the Second World War - by which time O.V.S. Bulleid had taken over from Maunsell - the 'Southern's carriage stock was in a parlous state, but Bulleid's plans were frustrated by post-war shortages of materials and the Southern Railway enlisted the help of outside contractors, notably the Birmingham Railway Carriage and Wagon Co. Bulleid's carriage designs featured large sidelights (windows) with bright and clean interiors that were much less fussy than pre-war types and metal fittings of chromed gun metal throughout. The most numerous type of vehicle built was the semi-open brake third corridor with 205 examples. Undoubtedly, Bulleid's best-remembered carriages, and certainly his most controversial, are the infamous Tavern cars and the accompanying Tavern trailers. These sets did not exactly find favour with the public and perhaps the less said about them the better! A total of 775 locomotive hauled passenger coaches (plus 38 catering vehicles) was built to Bulleid's design with many lasting on the SR until 1968. Small batches of open thirds were sent to the Scottish and Eastern regions in 1965 in exchange for Mk.1 coaches and some Bulleid vehicles are thought to have survived in traffic in Scotland as late as 1970. How strange it is that the last outpost of Southern Railway-designed loco-hauled passenger rolling stock appears to have been in Scotland!

Compilation of this book would not have been possible without the considerable help and advice of Ted Crawforth, Roger Merry-Price, Trevor Rapley and David Wigley, all of whom have provided extensive information about the vehicles depicted in this album, and wholehearted thanks are due to these gentlemen. Typesetting and design by Bruce Murray. I accept responsibility for any errors that have remained undetected. Publication of this book would not, of course, have been feasible without the co-operation of the various photographers, who had the foresight to photograph coaches and have subsequently trusted me with their precious transparencies. Many thanks! It has been suggested that this album is a railway publishing 'first' - surely not?

M.S.W. Burgess Hill, West Sussex, July 2010.

Coach No.S2626S and No.S4654S

Originating Company:	LSWR	**Type of Coach:**	Brake Third / Composite Lavatory
SR Diagram No:	98 / 285	**Build Date:**	1898 (S2626S) / 1902 (S4654S)
Length:	58ft 0in	**Seating Capacity:**	1st - 16 / 2nd - 22 (S2626S) / 1st - 16 / 2nd - 50 (S4654S)

The coaches depicted in this shot, which was taken at Evercreech Junction on 22 July 1958, are both of LSWR origin. The Southern Region was obliged to provide half of the rolling stock for Somerset and Dorset line local services and it is thought these carriages were stabled at Evercreech for use on the Highbridge branch, though in reality they were probably very rarely used. Seeing these two coaches depicted in their final form, it is hard to believe that they were constructed as two identical vehicles. The coach nearest to the camera is third brake No.2626, which was built as 48ft long bi-composite coach No.681 in November 1898. It was renumbered No.2820 in September 1915. When built this coach would have provided seats for 16 first and 22 second class passengers. Amazingly, no fewer than four lavatories were provided, two for the use of first class travellers and two for the second class passengers, but even so not all second class passengers had access to a toilet! Under the SR the carriage was renumbered 4684 in August 1926. It was withdrawn in October 1936 and a new 58ft underframe was fitted at Lancing works, the vehicle emerging as third brake No.2626, which was eventually withdrawn in July 1959. The coach furthest from the camera is No.4654, which like its sister vehicle was built with a 48ft long body, but in this case it was No.138 (later No.2381), built in May 1902. It was rebuilt on a 58ft long underframe in October 1936 with two additional third class compartments eliminating the former second class lavatories. Like No.2626 it was also withdrawn in July 1959. It is interesting to note that the summer 1955 carriage working appendix lists these two vehicles as 'loose' non-corridor carriages berthed at Templecombe for Somerset & Dorset services.

R.C. Riley

Coach No.DS1595 formerly LSWR No.540

Originating Company:	LSWR	**Type of Coach:**	Brake Third
SR Diagram No:	3119	**Build Date:**	1904
Length:	56ft 0in	**Seating Capacity:**	3rd - 32

A former LSWR brake third is seen at Hither Green on 17 March 1962 in departmental use. This coach was originally built in June 1904 as No.540 and was later renumbered No.1713 by the LSWR. When that railway was taken over by the Southern Railway it became No.3119 in their series. This coach was not destined to last long in passenger use on BR because it was transferred to departmental service as No.DS1595 in March 1951, allocated to the Ramsgate breakdown train unit as a mess and tool van. It was withdrawn from this role on 20 April 1963, but was commandeered for use as an internal user vehicle at Hither Green, becoming No.081632. It lasted in this lowly duty until 30 April 1966 when it was finally condemned.

Colour-Rail

Coach No.DS3198 and No.DS3210

Originating Company:	LSWR	**Type of Coach:**	Brake Third
SR Diagram No:	134 / 124	**Build Date:**	1921 (DS3198) / 1907 (DS3210)
Length:	57ft 0in / 56ft 0in	**Seating Capacity:**	3rd - 32 / 3rd - 38

In this picture, taken at Dover motive power depot on Sunday 6 March 1960, two vehicles allocated to the breakdown train await their next emergency assignment: both are very smart in crimson livery. That nearest the camera is No.DS3198 outshopped from Eastleigh carriage works as No. 1284 in December 1921. It bore this number for only a brief period, becoming Southern Railway No.3161 at the grouping and allocated to set No.339. Its career as a passenger-carrying coach came to an end on 5 January 1952, and it became No.DS3198 in the departmental series on 12 July 1952. It was finally withdrawn on 14 March 1964. The vehicle furthest from the photographer is No. DS3210, a carriage that was built in December 1907 as LSWR No.1455 and it became No.2956 after the Grouping. It was converted for service use, and also withdrawn, at exactly the same time as No.3198.

Rodney Lissenden

Coach No.S3190S

Originating Company:	LSWR	**Type of Coach:**	Brake Third Corridor
SR Diagram No:	135	**Build Date:**	1923
Length:	57ft 0in	**Seating Capacity:**	3rd - 32

Former LSWR 'Ironclad' brake third corridor No.3190, photographed from the corridor side, at Templecombe on 2 July 1959. These vehicles were immediately recognisable due to their very solid construction, steel sheeted exterior and, on the brake vehicles, recessed guards' compartment doors. The first of these coaches was constructed at Eastleigh in 1921, but this particular vehicle was built in 1923 and allocated to a five-coach set which later became set No.435. No.3190 was originally delivered as LSWR No.1353 and finished in LSWR sage green livery. No.3190, in accordance with LSWR practice, was a right handed brake coach, which means that viewed from the brake compartment the corridor was on the right hand side. In a five-car set the other brake vehicle was left handed. This carriage was one of the last vehicles built with LSWR double-framed Dreadnought bogies. From the time of its construction until the electrification of the Portsmouth Direct line in July 1937, No.3190 would have been allocated to main line Waterloo to Portsmouth and Bournemouth duties, but following completion of the Portsmouth electrification scheme, many of the 'Ironclad' sets were displaced and relegated to secondary services. No.3190 was still allocated to set No.435 in 1947 but now largely confined to special traffic duties. It was eventually condemned in July 1959, shortly after this view was taken, but its career was far from over. It was then converted for service use at Exmouth Junction and re-numbered DS70016 (later DW70016). In October 1978 it was sold to the Mid Hants Railway.

R.C. Riley

L & SWR

Coach No.1635S

Originating Company:	LBSCR	**Type of Coach:**	Non-corridor Composite
SR Diagram No:	360A	**Build Date:**	1906
Length:	56ft 0in	**Seating Capacity:**	1st - 24 / 3rd - 40

The first services using 'Balloon' coaches powered by a LBSCR 'Terrier' locomotive commenced in 1906 between Chichester and Portsmouth, Brighton and Seaford, Brighton and East Grinstead, and on various local duties around Horsham and Tunbridge Wells. In addition, the same combination covered purely local trains on the Epsom Downs branch and in the Brighton area. The introduction of these trains prompted the opening of many small, unstaffed halts, some of which had only a brief existence, while others survived on a long-term basis and are still in operation today. The rather decrepit coach seen here at Lancing works on 21 August 1963 was originally employed on the Brighton main line and was not converted for 'pull-push' operation until 1934, nearly thirty years after the LBSCR 'pull-push' 'balloon' coach concept was introduced. It was originally composite vehicle No.6271 and ran in set No.734 between 1934 and 1941. It was withdrawn from passenger service on 28 May 1941 but was subsequently used as a service vehicle. In 1935 this set was based at Bognor Regis, while in 1939 it was allocated to Horsham. The three first class compartments are in the middle of the carriage and can be clearly discerned, the third class accommodation being at each end. When built, the first class compartments seated six passengers and they were later modified to take four abreast, thus giving a total of eight. Owing to their very generous proportions, the 'Balloon' sets were given route restriction '5' by the Southern Railway and consequently rarely strayed off the former LBSCR lines, though the sets based at Horsham regularly worked to Guildford and on the Pulborough to Petersfield branch, where they were just over the 'border' on foreign territory.

Roy Hobbs

Coach No.S3821

Originating Company:	LBSCR		**Type of Coach:**	Driving Brake Third
SR Diagram No:	188		**Build Date:**	1912
Length:	54ft 0in		**Seating Capacity:**	3rd - 64

Coach No.3821, seen in this photograph in crimson lake livery on the rear of an Exeter to Salisbury local train at Axminster on 25 July 1959, was originally LBSCR No.1347, built in 1912 for use on the Eastbourne to St. Leonards service. The vehicle accommodated sixty-four passengers in open sided compartments without corridor partitions. When first built the driving end had only two small windows, but some time in the 1920s it was reconstructed with a standard driving end providing improved visibility. In 1922 coach No.1347 (as it then was) was paired with a trailer composite and by the following year was based at Horsham for use on services radiating from that town. By 1945 and still paired with its trailer composite, it could be found on the South Eastern section, but following the withdrawal of its sister coach, migrated to the South Western section where it usually worked with LSWR Third No.253. Between 1957 and 1959 it was noted at locations as far apart as Portsmouth and Exeter. It was withdrawn in October 1959.

R.C. Riley

Coach No.S3847S

Originating Company:	LBSCR	**Type of Coach:**	Driving Brake Third
SR Diagram No:	193	**Build Date:**	1921
Length:	54ft 0in	**Seating Capacity:**	3rd - 64

Following the end of wartime restrictions on construction, the LBSCR built four more two-coach pull-push sets, SR set Nos.981-984, supposedly for general use. Set No.982 consisted of driving brake third vehicle No.3847 (LBSCR No.1402) plus composite carriage No.6238, and in the 1924 working notices the set was shown as based at Horsham for services to Guildford, Three Bridges and Midhurst. In 1937 the set was renumbered 715 and during the following year vehicle No.6238 was removed and modified for use on the Isle of Wight, its replacement being SECR coach No.5298. The latter carriage was a non-corridor coach and the redundant corridor connection at the end of No.3847 was removed in 1939. In February 1952 the set was reformed again and No. 3847 became a loose vehicle - in effect a one-coach set - dedicated for use on the Pulborough-Midhurst-Petersfield line. When this route was closed in February 1955, No.3847 found little further employment, apart from regular sorties on the restored Lewes to East Grinstead service, until it was withdrawn in September 1960. No.3847 is seen here forming a Lewes to East Grinstead train leaving West Hoathly behind C2X Class 0-6-0 No.32440 on 13 March 1958. This particular coach had distinctive open-sided compartments, thus giving a passenger sitting on one of the former corridor end seats a view down the entire length of the carriage, a feature which no doubt added to the fascination of a journey along a line that had 'come back from the dead'.

R.C. Riley

Coach No.S3855S

Originating Company:	LBSCR	**Type of Coach:**	Driving Brake Third
SR Diagram No:	194	**Build Date:**	1922
Length:	54ft 0in	**Seating Capacity:**	3rd - 48

This vehicle, photographed at Westerham on an unknown date in the summer of 1960, was one of the last new 'pull-push' coaches authorised by the LBSCR. It was paired with composite coach No.6250 in set No.990 and originally intended for 'branch line service' and saw extensive use over the LBSCR's country lines. Internally, the coach had forty-eight seats, arranged in open compartments except that is at the inner end of the vehicle where two seats were provided on each side of the communicating door to the next carriage. The vehicle was especially notable because it had only six compartments, divided equally between smoking and non-smoking accommodation and consequently boasted a much larger brake van than previous designs. Note the different design of the door ventilators, and that the original mouldings have been hidden by steel panelling. In 1937 set No.990 was renumbered 723 and soon afterwards was exiled to the Seaton branch where a LBSCR 'pull-push' set must have been quite a novelty - it was certainly most unusual for such a set to be used so far westwards. The set remained on the Seaton branch until 1949 and henceforth found employment on the Central and Eastern sections until withdrawn in September 1960.

Barry Blacklock / Roy Denison collection

Coach No.DS3193 formerly SECR No.916

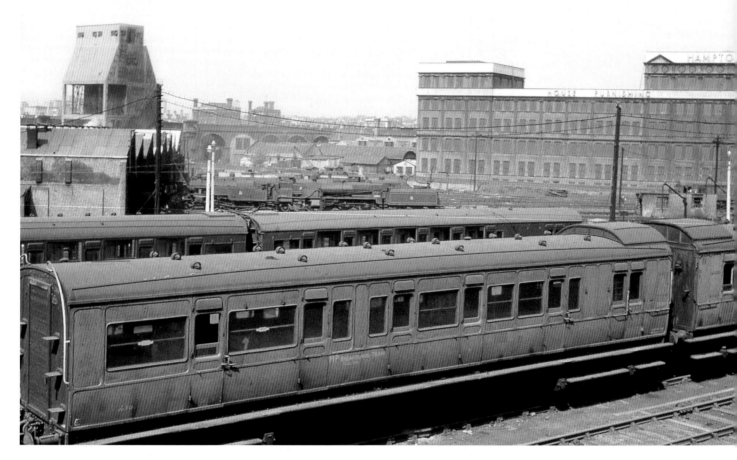

Originating Company:	SECR	Type of Coach:	Brake Composite Corridor
SR Diagram No:	423	Build Date:	1907
Length:	50ft 1in	Seating Capacity:	1st - 8 / 2nd - 6 / 3rd - 12

The huge coaling tower and massive bulk of Hampton's warehouse immediately identify the location of this picture; it is, of course, Stewarts Lane shed, Battersea, on the outskirts of London Victoria station. This photograph was taken on 10 May 1959 with the principal subject tool van No.DS3193 (SECR No.916), a vehicle of 1907 vintage. This was one of fifteen carriages (with detail differences) built at Ashford works mainly for employment on through services to the Midlands and north of England. No.916 was constructed for use on through trains to London & North Western Railway tracks. It was built with first, second and third class accommodation, access to which was from a side corridor, but this facility considerably restricted the width of the coach with the result that the first class compartments accommodated only four passengers while the second and third class had seating for six. The coach bodies were constructed of teak with mahogany panelling and mouldings. One aspect of the vehicles that probably amused passengers was the large number of doors per carriage, No.916 having no fewer than twenty-five. Unusually, hinged doors provided access from the corridor into the compartments. By SECR standards these vehicles were quite stylish and sister vehicle No.915 was displayed at the Franco-British Exhibition in 1908. In 1910 a coach of this type was included in the formation of the 10.15am Deal to Manchester London Road train and returned on the 10.10am Manchester to Deal the following day. In Southern Railway days No.916 underwent a change of identity and became No.6625, lasting in passenger traffic until December 1952. It was transferred to departmental use as No.DS3193 and was finally withdrawn in April 1965.

R.C. Riley

Coach No.DS3207 formerly SECR No.1050

Originating Company:	SECR	**Type of Coach:**	Composite Brake
SR Diagram No:	155	**Build Date:**	1909
Length:	50ft 1in	**Seating Capacity:**	2nd - 6 / 3rd - 50

Constructed by the Metropolitan Carriage, Wagon & Finance Co. in November 1909, coach No.DS3207 is seen at New Cross Gate in an extremely dilapidated condition on 1 October 1961, not many months before withdrawal. No.DS3207 was originally built as SECR No.1050, a composite brake consisting of one second class compartment (nearest the camera in this shot) and five third class compartments. This coach would have been used at first on SECR outer suburban services and was permanently formed in three coach set No.537 with a composite brake lavatory and composite lavatory vehicle. Note that the top panels are rounded in SECR style, while the bottom panels are square cornered reflecting LCDR practice. No.DS3207 lasted in ordinary passenger service (as No.S3323S) until January 1952 when it was taken out of service and converted for departmental use. It was finally condemned on 20 January 1962.

R.C. Riley

Coach No.AD5311 formerly SECR No.1100

Originating Company:	SECR	**Type of Coach:**	Brake Composite Lavatory
SR Diagram No:	158	**Build Date:**	1910
Length:	54ft 1in	**Seating Capacity:**	2nd - 7 / 3rd - 48

Seen here at Northiam, on the Kent & East Sussex Railway (K&ESR), on 25 June 1972, vehicle No.AD5311 first saw the light of day as SECR No.1100 at Ashford in 1910 and was allocated to three coach 'A' set No.113. Upon the formation of the Southern Railway in 1923, it was renumbered 3368 and used in set No.552, which was sold to the War Department in October 1943, No.3368 becoming WD No.13583. It was then based on the Longmoor Military Railway and used for passenger services until that establishment closed in October 1969. Latterly it had been known as No.AD5311. It was purchased by the K&ESR in September 1970, together with sister vehicle No.AD5312 and some repair work was undertaken on No.61 (as No.AD5311 was known on the K&ESR) thus enabling it to be used in passenger traffic for a number of years from 1974 onwards. Age plus wear and tear took their toll however, and No.61 was later withdrawn for an extensive overhaul to be undertaken. This work has now been completed and the coach returned to service. It is worth noting that in 1948/49 all eighteen surviving coaches of this type in BR service were converted to third class vehicles for use on the Isle of Wight. It should be noted that the guard's compartment was removed and two extra passenger compartments provided.

David Wigley

Coach No.DS136 formerly SECR No.1247

Originating Company:	SECR	**Type of Coach:**	Brake Composite Lavatory
SR Diagram No:	162	**Build Date:**	1913
Length:	60ft 1in	**Seating Capacity:**	2nd - 13 / 3rd - 40

This former semi-corridor vehicle, pictured at Clapham Yard on 26 April 1967, was constructed by Cravens of Darnall, Sheffield, in August 1913 and entered traffic as SECR No.1247. Originally it had two second and five third class compartments with two lavatories, one serving the second class accommodation while passengers in three of the five third class compartments had access to the other toilet. The position of the doors gives a good indication of the layout of the carriage. The vehicle ran in Trio 'C' set No.174. In Southern Railway days the carriage was renumbered 3511 and allocated to set No.606. It was withdrawn in June 1956 and later converted to the mobile laboratory seen here. The massive building towering behind the coach is Clapham Junction carriage berthing shed which is still in use at the time of writing.

David Wigley

Coach No.S5468S

Originating Company:	SECR	**Type of Coach:**	Composite Lavatory (with Saloon)
SR Diagram No:	316	**Build Date:**	1913
Length:	60ft 1in	**Seating Capacity:**	1st - 26 / 2nd - 24

This location, immediately north of Horsted Keynes station on the Bluebell Railway, will be familiar to many readers, but few are likely to have been lucky enough to witness a LBSCR K Class 'Mogul' departing with a northbound train. This really vintage scene shows the 3.28pm Haywards Heath to London Bridge train leaving behind No.32343 on 30 April 1955, shortly before the first withdrawal of passenger services. The carriage nearest to the camera is No.5468, built by the Metropolitan Amalgamated Railway Carriage & Wagon Co. which entered service in November 1913 as No.1216, a first and second class composite formed in set No.163. When the Southern Railway took over, it was renumbered No.5468 in July 1928, set No.163 becoming 595. This coach was clearly designed by somebody with a sense of humour, as despite the fact that two lavatories were provided, the arrangement of the passenger accommodation was such that only fourteen of the twenty-six first class passengers had access to a toilet, while none of the second class passengers, located in closed compartments, were able to reach one at all! Twelve of the first class seats were also in closed compartments. One of the lavatories was only accessible to a mere five passengers so was unlikely to have been frequently patronised. This coach was noteworthy because of the luxurious first class saloon seating which included four loose armchairs - what a contrast to the spartan and uncomfortable seating in today's modern trains! The first and second class accommodation can be identified by the figures (or lack of them) on the doors, while the saloon seating area has a large window. No.5468 was eventually withdrawn from traffic on 21 June 1958.

R.C. Riley

This picture shows SECR ten compartment third No.1055 in the sidings at Gatwick Airport in June 1962, awaiting its final call for breaking-up at Newhaven. This vehicle was one of 66 carriages put into traffic by the SECR in 1920/21, this particular coach officially recorded as being available for service from 15 August 1921. The body was constructed by the Birmingham Railway Carriage and Wagon Company of Smethwick while the underframe was built by Gloucester RCW Co. The coach entered traffic as SECR No.1373 subsequently becoming No.1055 under the SR. The wooden body was covered with two overlapping layers of sheet steel with standard SECR style commode handles. The extremely hard seats in these coaches qualify them as probably one of the most uncomfortable carriages pictured in this album, but this feature no doubt accounts for their popularity with passengers on the Bluebell Railway where two examples survive. No.1055 lasted in service until October 1961.   *Roy Hobbs*

Originating Company:	SECR	Type of Coach:	Non-corridor Third	**Coach Nos.S1055S**
SR Diagram No:	52	Build Date:	1921 (S1055S) / 1922 (S1087S)	**and S1087S**
Length:	60ft 1in	Seating Capacity:	3rd - 100	

This coach is basically the same as the vehicle depicted in the previous illustration but has some constructional and design differences. The body was built by the SECR at Ashford works, while the underframe was constructed by Birmingham RCW Co. The coach was originally numbered 1405 in the SECR series. Coaches in the 1084 to 1093 SR number series were built with steel panelling above the waist and matchboarding below. Another small design difference to the coach in the previous picture is the commode handles which had been recovered from withdrawn LCDR carriages. No.1087 was withdrawn from ordinary service in November 1959 but granted a stay of execution, because in January 1960 it was transferred to service use as No.DS70064 in the Lancing workmen's train. It was condemned in November 1963. No.1087 is seen here at Sidmouth on 24 July 1958 with its distinctive matchboarding clearly visible.   *R.C. Riley*

Coach No.S7380S

Originating Company:	SECR	**Type of Coach:**	First Corridor
SR Diagram No:	496 (later 54 as third corridor)	**Build Date:**	1924
Length:	62ft 0in	**Seating Capacity:**	1st - 26 (later 39 third)

This real gem of a photograph shows 'Continental' coach No.7380 in (what appears to be) Southern Railway malachite green livery at Ashford in 1954. This vehicle was one of eight identical carriages (Nos.7376 to 7383) constructed by the Birmingham Railway Carriage and Wagon Company in 1924 in preference to the SR's own workshops, as the former could promise much quicker delivery, the Southern being desperate for more boat train stock at that time. These coaches differed from 'Continental' vehicles ordered by the SECR, due to their increased width - they were 8ft. 6½in. wide as opposed to the previous 'standard' 8ft. 0¾in. width for this type of stock. The carriages were distinguished by their inward opening doors, although later it was felt these were a hazard to passengers and in late SR / early BR days the doors were altered to outward opening, distinguished by kinked handrails to prevent passengers from hurting their hands. The coach seen here appears to retain the old arrangement. In June 1954 (the shot seen here was presumably taken before that time), No.7380 was downgraded to third class with 39 seats, renumbered 647, and transferred to set No.261 for Eastern Section special traffic duties. In the mid-1950s this set reportedly formed the 8.06 am Victoria to Margate and 3.34pm return on summer Saturdays only, hardly worthwhile employment. Apart from two specimens destroyed by enemy action, most of the 'Continental' first class vehicles were condemned in 1958/59, No.7380 going in September 1958.

Colour-Rail

Coach No.1001, seen here (nearest to the camera) at Gatwick Airport sidings awaiting disposal on 26 June 1960, was one of twelve second class 'Continental' vehicles ordered in October 1923. No.1001 originally entered traffic as second corridor vehicle No.4173 with seating for forty-five passengers in seven and a half compartments, but in 1934 in response to an increasing demand for third class travel, all second class 'Continental' coaches were downgraded to third and renumbered accordingly. These coaches were quite distinctive with their inward opening doors, long commode handles and matchboarded bodysides. Phase One of the Kent Coast Electrification from London to Ramsgate and Dover rendered most of the 'Continental' coaches redundant, No.1001 being withdrawn in August 1959, but fortunately brake third corridor No.3554 survived into preservation on the Keighley and Worth Valley Railway. The three vehicles to which No.1001 is attached are also 'Continental' coaches.

Colour-Rail

Coach Nos.S1001S and S782S

Originating Company:	SECR	**Type of Coach:**	Third Corridor	
SR Diagram No:	235 (2002 after downgrading)	**Build Dates:**	1924 (S1001) / 1927 (S782S)	
Length:	62ft 0in	**Seating Capacity:**	3rd - 45	

This carriage was one of the final ten 'Continental' vehicles (six Firsts and four Thirds) ordered by the SR in November 1926 and built to the 8ft. 6½in. 'Restriction 1' width. No.782 entered traffic in October 1927 and, many years later, was photographed at Eardley Road carriage sidings on 30 October 1960 with sister vehicle No.780 also visible. These vehicles seated 45 passengers in seven full-size compartments seating six passengers, plus a coupe compartment with seats for three which is nearest to the camera in this illustration. There is some uncertainty regarding the origin of this batch of vehicles, but the official record indicates that both the body and underframe of coach No.782 were built at Eastleigh. The records state that the underframe of No.783, however, was built by Metropolitan Cammell and only the body was constructed at Eastleigh. No.782 was redesignated 'second' in June 1956 and subsequently survived in special traffic set No.212 to become one of the last 'Continental' coaches in use, most of this stock having been withdrawn in 1957/59. No.782 was finally withdrawn on 3 June 1961.

R.C. Riley

Coach No.S4043S

Originating Company:	SR	**Type of Coach:**	Brake Third Corridor
SR Diagram No:	137	**Build Date:**	1925
Length:	57ft 0in	**Seating Capacity:**	3rd - 48

In this picture of Horsted Keynes dump, taken on 27 September 1959, three vehicles are seen awaiting their fate - note the 'hot cross bun' condemnation branding. The middle carriage is 'Ironclad' brake third No.4043 constructed in 1925 for use in 11-coach set No.471 on the Brighton to London Bridge and return 'City Limited'. It was also one of the last vehicles to be built at Lancing carriage works which henceforth concentrated on building underframes and overhauls. The 'City Limited' was patronised mainly by wealthy businessmen hence the amount of third class accommodation provided was small compared to the first class. Note that the coach was equipped with 9ft. wheelbase plate framed bogies in contrast to coach No.3190 which is seen in a previous illustration. Following the Brighton Line Electrification, set No.471 was reduced to four coaches only, with coach No.4043 being transferred to set No.465. Vehicle No.4043 survived until August 1959 when it was withdrawn from traffic, made redundant by the inauguration of Phase One of the Kent Coast Electrification scheme.

Colour-Rail

Coach No.S1050S

Originating Company:	SER (body) / SR (underframe)	**Type of Coach:**	Non-corridor Third
SR Diagram No:	90	**Build Dates:**	Body sections circa 1880 / Underframe 1927
Length:	62ft 6in	**Seating Capacity:**	3rd - 100

This coach, seen at Seaton Junction on 24 July 1958, probably has the most interesting and complex history of any vehicle featured in this album. It was described as an 'Electric Conversion Pattern Coach' and has an underframe of the electric standard 62ft. 6in. length, 4ft. 6in. longer than contemporary steam stock. It appears to have been used to demonstrate the principles for the conversion of steam stock to multiple unit suburban electrics at Ashford works. Officially, it is formed of two SECR coach bodies from vehicle Nos.568 and 792 mounted on a new underframe, but examination has revealed that there are three different compartment widths, which suggests that bodies from more than two vehicles may have been used in its construction. It is also possible that the skilled craftsmen at Ashford works may have constructed the middle section on an *ad hoc* basis without drawings. No.1050 was released to traffic in 1927 as composite No.5546, but in 1943 it was demoted to third class, re-numbered, and fitted with pull-push through pipes for use as a strengthening vehicle on the Seaton and Swanage branch lines. It remained there until displaced by more modern coaches in the early 1960s. Upon withdrawal it was sent to the Ardingly 'dump' from where it was rescued by the Bluebell Railway, arriving on Bluebell metals in May 1963. No.1050 was used intensively on the Bluebell Railway in the 1960s but was withdrawn from service in the early 1970s and, regrettably, has since been stored out of use. The true origin of this total oddity will probably never be known and it remains something of a mystery coach.

R.C. Riley

Coach No.081256 formerly SR No.7216

Originating Company:	SR	**Type of Coach:**	First Corridor
SR Diagram No:	2501	**Build Date:**	1927
Length:	59ft 0in	**Seating Capacity:**	1st - 42

Many redundant coaches were used as offices in past times and they could be seen dotted around the system at a variety of locations. These vehicles were generally numbered in the internal user series, which denoted that they were allocated for static use at a particular location. This specimen is internal user No.081256, a familiar sight at Chichester for many years. It was photographed there on 20 September 1968, by which date and judging by the broken window, it was already out of use. The vehicle began life in 1927. It is thought the entire vehicle was built by the Midland Railway Carriage & Wagon Co. at Birmingham. It was one of a dozen first class corridor carriages (Nos.7216 to 7227), constructed for use on the Waterloo to Southampton boat trains and seated 42 passengers in seven compartments. There were lavatories at each end of the coach. It featured the low height corridor side sidelights that were typical of the early Maunsell stock. Withdrawn from ordinary traffic in September 1959 and after several years use at Chichester it was broken up on site in July 1969.

David Wigley

Coach No.S3705S

Originating Company:	SR	**Type of Coach:**	Brake Third Corridor
SR Diagram No:	2104	**Build Date:**	1931
Length:	59ft 0in	**Seating Capacity:**	3rd - 48

Judging by its immaculate appearance, Maunsell third brake No.3705 appears to have been just released from a heavy overhaul when photographed at New Cross Gate on 1 October 1961. One can almost smell that new paint! This carriage was ordered in July 1929 for use in four coach set No.189 on the Victoria to Eastbourne/Hastings services. It seated forty-eight passengers in six third class compartments. This coach was destined to remain in set No.189 throughout most of its life, as evidenced here by the set number prominently displayed on the end of the vehicle. In 1962 a decision was taken to split up many of the remaining sets, and in June 1963 coach No.3705 found itself in two coach set No.189. It was eventually withdrawn from service in March 1965 following the dieselisation of the Reading to Tonbridge service.

Rodney Lissenden

Coach No.S3690S

Originating Company:	SR	**Type of Coach:**	Brake Third Corridor
SR Diagram No:	2105	**Build Date:**	1931
Length:	59ft 0in	**Seating Capacity:**	3rd - 36

Maunsell brake third corridor coach No.3690 was photographed at Eardley Road carriage sidings, near Streatham, on 30 October 1960. This vehicle was one of a batch of 8ft. 0¾in. wide carriages ordered in June 1929 for use on the London to Bexhill West and Hastings services. The order was for two nine-coach trains but the coaches were actually delivered as four three-coach sets and six loose vehicles, these being outshopped in January and February 1931. Coach No.3690 was originally allocated to set No.216 which was an 'F set' with the unusual formation of two brake thirds flanking a first. It was recorded as running as a loose vehicle in June 1960, being one of the few Hastings gauge 'Restriction 0' coaches retained for newspaper trains after the full implementation of the Hastings line dieselisation scheme. The passenger compartments were 6ft. 3in. wide and the guards' brake compartment was 16ft. 6¾in long. Coach No.3690 remained in traffic for another year after this picture was taken, being withdrawn on 7 October 1960.

R.C. Riley

Coach No.S4440S

Originating Company:	SR		**Type of Coach:**	Un-classed General Saloon Brake
SR Diagram No:	2654		**Build Date:**	1933
Length:	59ft 0in		**Seating Capacity:**	Un-classed

Coach No.4440 was one of twenty general saloons intended for boat train traffic built in 1933, commonly known as 'Nondescript Brakes'. These carriages were generally used as first class for race traffic, second class on boat trains and third class for schools traffic or excursions, so they were very versatile carriages. Six seating bays were provided each accommodating six with four passengers on one side of the central aisle and two on the other. The luxurious seats, all with individual armrests, were similar to armchairs and every passenger had plenty of room to move. One lavatory compartment was provided. This photograph was taken at Horsted Keynes on 1 April 1962 when the vehicle was forming part of a rail tour to the Bluebell Railway. It was withdrawn from service in December 1963.

Colour-Rail

Coach No.S6686S

Originating Company:	SR	**Type of Coach:**	Brake Composite Corridor
SR Diagram No:	2403	**Build Date:**	1935
Length:	59ft 0in	**Seating Capacity:**	1st - 12 / 3rd - 32

Maunsell brake composite corridor coach No.6686 is depicted berthed at Fareham on 27 July 1969. By the date of this picture No.6686 had been secured for preservation but was still largely in BR condition. This is one of twenty-five coaches of this type ordered in March 1934 for Waterloo to West-of-England services and this particular example was out-shopped in September 1935. These vehicles had the same internal layout as earlier designs but were rather different externally with steel panelling screwed onto the wooden superstructure, large radius corners to the windows and frameless droplights. The droplights were secured with a locking mechanism operated by a lever with 'free' and 'secure' indications and there were instructions on how to open the window. The layout of the external doors was also different in that on the corridor side the doors were placed between compartments rather than in line with the internal compartment doors. In February 1960 No.6686 had the good fortune to be fitted with electric heating, in addition to its existing steam heating, thus making the coach (in BR parlance) dual heated. It was one of three similar carriages allocated to the London to Paris 'Night Ferry' service and survived as late as September 1966. It was purchased for preservation by the Southern Locomotive Preservation Co. Ltd., and initially stored at Droxford on the former Meon Valley line. It was transferred to the Bluebell Railway on 2 October 1971 and has since received a comprehensive overhaul in their Horsted Keynes workshops.

David Wigley

Coach No.081642 formerly SR No.1309

Originating Company:	SR	**Type of Coach:**	Open Saloon Third
SR Diagram No:	2007	**Build Date:**	1935
Length:	59ft 0in	**Seating Capacity:**	3rd - 56

Maunsell open third coach No.1309 is depicted in use as a work study office at Woking on 10 August 1969, by which time it had been renumbered in the Internal User series as 081642. This coach was ordered in April 1933, and delivered in 1935, as part of a batch of thirty open saloon coaches for general use and these vehicles are widely considered to be one of Maunsell's most attractive designs. They represented a radical break from earlier coach design and had exterior steel panelling screwed onto the framework that was flush with the windows, thus giving a much cleaner, less cluttered appearance, but the traditional wooden-framed door droplights were retained. The coaches were fitted with 'Airstream' ventilators which, it was claimed at the time, emitted fresh air without draughts and prevented grit from entering the carriage interior. Internally, luggage racks were fitted in the spaces opposite the lavatories at each end of the coach and the seating was divided into three separate saloons, the middle one consisting of twenty-four seats while the others were sixteen seat saloons. Condemned on 8 December 1962, No.1309 was converted into a mobile office and saw use at Eastleigh, Woking and Brockenhurst in this guise before being withdrawn for scrap in 1971. It was, however, rescued in late 1972 by the Southern Coaching Stock Preservation Group and was delivered to the Bluebell Railway on 1 March 1973. It was fully restored at the Bluebell, entering traffic there on 2 December 1984, and remains in service at the time of writing.

David Wigley

Coach No.S7679S

Originating Company:	SR	**Type of Coach:**	Restaurant First
SR Diagram No:	2507	**Build Date:**	1947
Length:	64ft 6in	**Seating Capacity:**	1st - 18 (compartments.) / 24 (saloon)

Eleven of these vehicles were built between August 1947 and March 1948 and the illustration depicts vehicle No.7679 at Droxford station, on the former Meon Valley line, on 16 September 1967. This carriage had been purchased by the Sadler Rail Coach Company, whose experimental railbus can be seen in the background, but sadly the coach was later scrapped after being vandalised and an example of this very distinctive design was lost. These cars were the matching vehicles to the third class kitchen cars and usually ran with the dining saloon, which is at the far end of the coach in this picture, adjacent to the kitchen car. The layout of the carriages was most unusual featuring both saloon (with loose chairs) and compartment accommodation in a similar fashion to Bulleid's brake third coaches. The first class compartments were quite well appointed with the seats trimmed with uncut green upholstery matched by green Rexine blinds. When new the compartments were fitted with a beige rug with a green border bearing the company's monogram. Panelling was of veneered East Indian satinwood with Indian silver greywood banding. The saloons, which had three-a-side seating, featured sidewalls covered with white rexine, while the green silk curtains and maroon carpet completed the furnishings. By far the most interesting aspect of the new vehicles was the lighting, these coaches being the first production series of British main line carriages to be equipped with fluorescent lighting.

Colour-Rail

Coach No. not known. S4209S to S4228S series

Originating Company:	SR	**Type of Coach:**	Brake Third Corridor
SR Diagram No:	2124	**Build Date:**	1947/48
Length:	64ft 6in	**Seating Capacity:**	3rd - 44

The Southern was keen to introduce new rolling stock as speedily as possible at the end of the Second World War but its plans were upset by materials shortages and a lack of production capacity at Lancing and Eastleigh works. Consequently, it was decided to approach outside contractors and the Birmingham Railway Carriage and Wagon Company (BRCW) was asked to build twenty-four 3-coach sets of Bulleid design at a cost not exceeding £19,000 per set; any costs over and above that figure would have been met by the government. An initial order for ten 3-coach sets was placed in February 1946 and other orders soon followed. Delivery was very slow, however, the first vehicles being completed in December 1947. This was not the fault of the contractors, but due to a shortage of materials that also affected production in the railway's own workshops. The unidentified brake third corridor vehicle seen here at Kensington (Olympia) on 27 August 1964, forming part of the Post Office workers' train to Clapham Junction, was one of the distinctive first batch of coaches ordered which had a coupe compartment adjacent to guard's van. Twenty of these vehicles were constructed and were allocated to set Nos.795 to 804. The BRCW-built coaches were very different to their SR counterparts in many respects, the most noticeable external difference being the use of Alpax alloy window frames that were 3in. shallower than on the Eastleigh stock and proud of the bodyside panelling. The sliding toplights were also shallower than those of the standard SR coaches although corridors were fitted with plain glass only without any sliding ventilators at all. These vehicles had galvanised panelling cut to much smaller dimensions than the Eastleigh coaches, this being screwed directly on to the wooden framing. The BRCW vehicles also had flat louvred casings on the roof rather than torpedo ventilators. Internally, the vehicles were reminiscent of the Maunsell era, particularly the seats which were almost identical to those of the mid-1930s. Unlike the SR carriages which had stainless steel kickplates and wood veneers to cantrail level, the BRCW vehicles were fitted with wooden kickplates painted brown plus rexine to waist level with wooden veneers above. The lighting was, however, a radical improvement on SR practice with bulbs concealed in ornate glass bowls in preference to rudimentary bare bulbs with reflectors. The toilet on the BRCW coaches was at the far end of the saloon adjacent to the end vestibule: there was a luggage rack opposite. Vehicle No.4211 is preserved on the Mid Hants Railway. Sister coach No.4227 exists in an unrestored condition at the Bluebell Railway.

Colour-Rail

Coach No.S5768S

Originating Company:	SR	**Type of Coach:**	Composite Corridor
SR Diagram No:	2318	**Build Date:**	1947
Length:	64ft 6in	**Seating Capacity:**	1st - 24 / 3rd - 24

Bulleid composite corridor coach No.5768 was ordered as part of a very ambitious building programme for 310 main line coaches agreed by the Southern Railway's Rolling Stock Committee in 1945. Not surprisingly, in view of the shortage of raw materials at the end of the Second World War, drawing up a construction schedule proved to be the easy part of the job and the actual building of the vehicles took a trifle longer than anticipated, with delivery of some coaches being delayed until 1949! No.5768 was one of a series of twenty-four identical carriages earmarked for use on Waterloo-Weymouth/Exeter services. It was delivered in 1947 and allocated to set No.787 where it remained (as far as is known) until the policy of allocating vehicles to specific sets was abandoned in early 1966. No.5768's passenger accommodation consists of four first and three third class compartments separated by a transverse vestibule. Lavatories were provided at each end of the coach. It was destined to survive until relatively late in the annals of Bulleid stock, not being withdrawn until October 1968. It was purchased by the Bulleid Society for a proposed museum at the Longmoor Military Railway but when that project collapsed it was moved to the Bluebell Railway where it arrived in late September 1971. It was restored for passenger use and was included in the train when *Blackmore Vale* (also owned by the Bulleid Society) returned to steam in May 1976. Apart from routine maintenance it remained in regular use at the Bluebell until being withdrawn from traffic due to body corrosion and other defects in 1993. It was stored out of use under tarpaulins for many years but in late 2009 was retrieved from the back siding, examined, and selected for a comprehensive overhaul at Horsted Keynes. No.5768 is pictured at Clapham Yard in late 1967 with the corridor side nearest to the camera. Note the shallower pattern sliding toplights with which many early Bulleid carriages were fitted. An identical coach, No.5761, is also preserved.

Tim Robbins

Coach No.DS70262 formerly SR No.1457

Originating Company:	SR	**Type of Coach:**	Open Saloon Third
SR Diagram No:	2017	**Build Dates:**	1948
Length:	64ft 6in	**Seating Capacity:**	3rd - 64

How the mighty have fallen! When DS70262 was out-shopped in early 1948 as No.1457 it was formed in one of the prestigious Bournemouth dining six-sets which offered (apart from Pullman cars) the highest standards of passenger comfort and amenity. The coach ends were painted green and the carriages boasted chromium plated handrails, so these sets stood out as really special. No.1457 was relegated to a special traffic set in 1964 and was withdrawn from ordinary passenger service in September 1966. In March 1967 it was converted for departmental use as a tunnel inspection coach, becoming DS70262, and is pictured at Stewarts Lane on 8 July 1985. Another characteristic that distinguished the vehicles allocated to the six car sets was the fact that the steel panelling was extended down to the bottom of the solebars, as seen here, but No.DS70262 appears to have had a small section in the middle removed to facilitate the fitting of a handbrake. The four openings beneath some windows are gas fire ventilators.

R.C. Riley

Coach No.S4363S

Originating Company:	SR	Type of Coach:	Brake Third Corridor
SR Diagram No:	2123	Build Date:	1948
Length:	64ft 6in	Seating Capacity:	3rd - 48

Bulleid semi-open brake third No.4363, photographed from the compartment side, is seen at Clapham Junction in about August 1967. This coach was originally constructed for use in one of the six-coach Bournemouth dining sets (set Nos.290 to 300) that were introduced solely for use on the prestigious Waterloo to Bournemouth service. These sets never worked to Exeter on a regular basis. The sets comprised of a semi-open brake third, a composite corridor vehicle with the third class next to the brake coach, a restaurant first with a dining saloon, a kitchen and third class dining saloon, an open third coach and another semi-open brake third. Great care was taken regarding the layout of the sets to ensure, for example, that no passenger had to walk very far to gain access to a lavatory. The sets had a particularly luxurious and opulent air which was emphasised by their solebar fairings, green-painted coach ends and chromium-plated handrails. This was the first time on the 'Southern' that catering vehicles were specifically allocated to fixed formation sets. Coach No.4363 was formed in set No.297 which entered traffic in January 1948. The passenger accommodation comprised a four bay saloon with seating for thirty-two, and two compartments each seating eight passengers. The saloon and compartments were separated by a gangway and toilet, the location of the latter, virtually in the middle of the coach, was quite unusual. No.4363 remained on the Bournemouth line until withdrawn from traffic in September 1967. This type of coach was the most numerous Bulleid design, no fewer that 205 examples being constructed and, fortunately, a number of these distinctive carriages have been preserved.

Tim Robbins

Coach No.S5789S

Originating Company:	SR	**Type of Coach:**	Composite Corridor
SR Diagram No:	2320	**Build Dates:**	1948
Length:	64ft 6in	**Seating Capacity:**	1st - 24 / 3rd - 24

This photograph of Bulleid composite corridor coach No.5789 was taken whilst it was berthed in Clapham yard in August 1967. This vehicle was ordered from the Birmingham Railway Carriage & Wagon Co. Ltd. in 1946, and was part of various orders that were placed by the Southern Railway with the company during the early months of that year. Altogether thirty-five sets were ordered up to July 1946 and, at that time, it was the intention that delivery would commence later that year. In the event this schedule proved to be very optimistic because construction was bedevilled by shortages of materials and No.5789 did not actually enter service until October 1948. This coach consisted of four first and three third class compartments and lavatories were provided at each end of the carriage. The corridor side is depicted in this photograph and the lack of sliding toplights is immediately noticeable, but BRCW Co. would no doubt claim that lack of ventilation in the corridors was compensated for by the much larger than normal air intakes on the roof. When built the coach would have been painted in malachite green livery and it is not thought that any of these coaches were ever repainted in crimson lake and cream before being repainted in SR green. Little is known about the wanderings of this particular vehicle in traffic, but it was formed in set No.809 for many years, together with brake third corridor vehicles Nos.4257 and 4258, and operated on the South Western Section. Coach No.5789 outlasted many of its sister vehicles and was eventually withdrawn from service in January 1968.

Tim Robbins

Bulleid Third corridor coach No.27 was ordered as part of the 1945 programme of construction and eventually built in January 1949 and allocated to set No.81, which was one of fifteen four-coach sets earmarked for use on London to Dover/Ramsgate services. The formation of this set would have included two semi-open brake third coaches and a seven compartment composite in addition to No.27. These sets were the last to be out-shopped in malachite green livery, but the first to be fitted with the 15in. deep sliding toplights (window ventilators). Presumably the shallower 10½in. pattern ventilators had not provided sufficient fresh air on hot summer days! When they were introduced these sets immediately appeared on the faster Kent coast services and remained on the London to Ramsgate via Faversham trains until Phase One of the Kent coast electrification scheme was inaugurated in June 1959. Thereafter they were confined to the London-Dover-Ramsgate-Margate services where some trains remained diesel-hauled until full electric working was implemented in June 1962. Subsequently it is likely that No.27 may have worked on the Central Section for a while before being moved to the South Western lines where it ended its days being withdrawn in January 1968. It is seen in this picture, photographed from the compartment side, at Clapham Yard in 1967.

Tim Robbins

Originating Company:	SR	**Type of Coach:**	Third Corridor	**Coach Nos.S27S**
SR Diagram No:	2019	**Build Date:**	1949 (S27S) / 1950 (S63S)	**and S63S**
Length:	64ft 6in	**Seating Capacity:**	3rd - 64	

Third Corridor No.63, which was photographed at Bournemouth Central in the mid-1960s, was one of forty coaches of this type ordered in August 1947 for use on the South Eastern Section and this vehicle was built in June 1950. The corridor side is depicted in this picture and note that some compartment doors and mirrors can just be discerned. The coach appears to have been re-sheeted at some stage - note the vertical steel panelling. This coach lasted until the end of steam on the Waterloo to Weymouth line and was withdrawn in July 1967.

Inter-Air Press

Coach No.S7615

Originating Company:	SR	**Type of Coach:**	First Corridor
SR Diagram No:	2552	**Build Date:**	1949
Length:	64ft 6in	**Seating Capacity:**	1st - 42

Bulleid First corridor No.7615, seen here at Bournemouth West on 21 July 1951, was one of forty vehicles constructed for use on the Dover and Southampton boat trains. It certainly makes a splendid sight in crimson and cream livery: note the coach number in the original position on the left hand side of the vehicle and that the number does not carry a suffix. These carriages seated forty-two passengers in seven compartments arranged in groups of three and four either side of a transverse vestibule. Two more vestibules were provided, one at each end of the coach, plus a pair of toilets at one end only. In the early 1950s No.7615 was allocated to first-class-only set No.356 but this set was infrequently used and soon disbanded, No.7615 thereafter spending the greater part of its career as a loose vehicle. No.7615 was eventually withdrawn from traffic on 26 June 1965.

Colour-Rail

Coach No.S7893S

Originating Company:	SR	**Type of Coach:**	Kitchen and Buttery Car (later Kitchen Buffet Car)
SR Diagram No:	2663 (2668 when rebuilt)	**Build Date:**	1949 (rebuilt 1959/60)
Length:	64ft 6in	**Seating Capacity:**	2nd - 12 (11 after rebuilding)

Tavern car No.7893, named *The Jolly Tar*, is seen at Exeter Central on 15 August 1957. The adjacent vehicle, which is partially visible, appears to be a converted tavern trailer: the tavern cars ran as sets with one of those vehicles. O.V.S. Bulleid was nothing if not a highly unconventional designer, and it would be something of an understatement to say that the tavern cars were one of the most remarkable flights of fantasy that has ever taken to the rails. In 1945 the Southern Railway Board authorised the building of eight two-coach sets for the Waterloo to West of England trains comprising a restaurant car and a composite dining saloon. The vehicles did not enter traffic until 1949 by which time the original specification for a restaurant car had been altered so that the sets now included a kitchen buffet car. Marylebone instructed that the new vehicles must be painted in the new BR colours, but apart from that the SR engineers were given a free hand regarding the interior design which proved rather innovative to say the least. The kitchen buffet cars were actually constructed as tavern cars, this idea apparently being inspired by a chance conversation under a cedar tree at the Botleigh Grange Hotel, Botley, Hampshire, where the SR hierarchy held lunchtime meetings. The word 'tavern' is defined as 'a public house for the supply of food and drink' and those present at the hotel evidently thought it would be a jolly good idea to incorporate a really cosy and inviting 'olde worlde' bar in a railway buffet car. To some degree the plans ran riot and while the buttery part of the cars was painted in the new cream and crimson lake livery the design team adopted a brickwork pattern for the lower half of the tavern section of the vehicles, allegedly to maintain the 'olde worlde' illusion. The top half was painted cream as specified by Marylebone, but the panelling was broken by vertical black beams to resemble an old timbered inn. The external paint scheme proved a big mistake, the outside appearance of the cars provoking much criticism from staff who dubbed them 'doll's houses'. Internally there were seasoned dark oak roof beams, 'whitewashed' ceilings and small imitation leaded windows, while square metal lanterns dangled from the ceiling. Flooring consisted of typical black and red country inn style tiling. In contrast at the kitchen end of the tavern was a modern cocktail bar and snack counter, the bar itself being faced with polished light oak. Unlike the rest of the coach the kitchen equipment was fairly conventional and perhaps it should also be mentioned that forced air ventilation was fitted. When the cars entered service they were featured briefly on Movietone News which stated that their introduction was 'cheerful news' and referred to the vehicles as 'pubs on wheels', suggesting that the idea could be extended. On 25 May 1949 senior BR officials inspected a Tavern set at Waterloo and it was announced that six sets would go into service on the 'Atlantic Coast Express' and on the Eastern and London Midland regions. By that date two sets were already running in two 'ACE' sets and a subsequent change of plan resulted in six sets being concentrated on the ER for use on its high profile named expresses, such as 'The Norfolkman' and 'The Master Cutler'. The introduction of the tavern car sets on the ER provoked howls of protest and passengers apparently boycotted the dining car (tavern trailer), which had less seating capacity than the coaches formerly used, and receipts nose dived as a result. Letters of protest were even sent to the Minister of Transport and in the face of such stiff opposition BR capitulated and by early 1950 tavern trailer coach No.7836 had arrived at Eastleigh for extensive rebuilding. The work entailed installation of orthodox windows and the fitting of tables and loose chairs in the first class section on traditional lines. All of the tavern trailer cars, which were later re-classified restaurant composite open (RCO), were similarly treated between June 1950 and June 1951, just in time for the start of the peak summer timetable. In June 1957 the first tavern car was repainted in green livery and two years later vehicle Nos.7892/96 were sent to Eastleigh carriage works for a complete overhaul that included reconstruction as conventional kitchen buffet cars with considerable use of laminated formica panelling, full depth sidelights (windows) and seating on each side of a central aisle. The introduction of BR Standard catering vehicles, and use of open second coaches for dining purposes, in the early 1960s led to a re-arrangement of some tavern car sets and withdrawal of RCOs commenced in 1965. The last of the tavern vehicles survived in traffic until late 1967, thus bringing to a close the careers of some of the most controversial carriages ever built in Great Britain.

Colour-Rail

Coach Nos.S1496S, E1486S and DS70314 formerly SR No.1482

Originating Company:	SR	**Type of Coach:**	Open Saloon Third
SR Diagram No:	2017	**Build Date:**	1951 (S1496S & E1486S) / 1950 (DS70314)
Length:	64ft 6in	**Seating Capacity:**	3rd - 64

Bulleid Open Third No.1496 is pictured at Longmoor Downs on 8 June 1968 in the formation of 'The Bulleid Commemorative Rail Tour'. The seating areas consisted of two saloons separated by a central vestibule, while there were other vestibules at each end of the coach, one of which gave access to two lavatories, one on each side of the gangway. The open thirds were the last surviving locomotive-hauled Bulleid vehicles in ordinary passenger service on the Southern Region, lasting until November 1968, and will probably be familiar to many readers. Forty-five of these coaches were constructed and they were completed between November 1950 and January 1951. All of the vehicles had entered service by June 1951, coach No.1496 being formed initially in set No.353 which was allocated exclusively to Waterloo-Southampton Docks boat trains. In 1954 the Bulleid vehicles in this set were replaced by new BR Standard coaches, and coach No.1496 became a loose vehicle for some time before being allocated to South Western Division special traffic set No.770 in 1964. It survived to become one of the very last Bulleid carriages in operation in the south of England, not being taken out of traffic until 21 September 1968. It should be noted that an earlier batch of open thirds was built in 1947/48 for the Bournemouth six-car dining sets and these carriages had detail differences, most notably the fairings which were extended over the solebar thus giving the coaches a very distinctive appearance. These coaches had fixed tables and were classified restaurant third open (RTO).

David Wigley

SR

A Bulleid coach in fully lined out maroon livery! In the mid-1960s a number of Bulleid vehicles were transferred to other regions, the largest batch being a total of 43 Brake Third Corridor and Brake Composite Corridor vehicles that were inherited by the Western Region in the 1963 regional boundary changes. In 1965 some Open Thirds (classified Open Seconds by that time) were sent to the Eastern and Scottish Regions in exchange for Mk.1 coaches earmarked for conversion to electric stock in connection with the Bournemouth electrification scheme. In this illustration coach No.1486 is seen, in absolutely sparkling external condition, at Stratford on 21 August 1965 coupled to another vehicle of the same type. The Southern Region had been required to repaint these

coaches in maroon before transfer. The Bulleid carriages were usually employed on secondary or relief services, but on 12 September 1965 Nos.1474 and 1505 were noted in the formation of the 9.36am Liverpool Street to Cambridge train and 9.05pm return. It was reported that they retained their SR maps! It is thought coach No.1486 remained in traffic at least until the following year, while some of those on the Scottish Region lasted much longer, the last survivors apparently being Nos.1466 and 1502, both of which were eventually withdrawn in February 1970. Presumably by that time they had become the last remaining Bulleid locomotive-hauled passenger vehicles in BR service.

Colour-Rail

Strange though it may seem, one of the last Bulleid coaches in BR use was DS70314 which survived as a carriage cleaning staff changing/mess room at Bellahouston carriage sidings, Glasgow, until withdrawn (assuming the markings on the body are correct) in March 1972. The figure '7654' on the coach side is the BR code number for the local carriage & wagon depot, presumably Bellahouston. This coach originally entered traffic in 1950 as No.1482 and spent much of its BR career as a loose vehicle, though it was allocated to sets for short periods. It led an unremarkable career until transferred to the Scottish Region in January 1966 in exchange for BR Standard vehicles that were earmarked for conversion to electric stock (4-REP/4-TC/3-TC) for use on the Waterloo to Bournemouth main line; prior to transfer it was repainted in maroon at Eastleigh works and relettered Sc1482S. The author can recall travelling in a similar coach (perhaps it was No.1482!) formed in a Glasgow Buchanan Street to Aberdeen relief on Good Friday 1966. Bizarrely, it is thought that the final Bulleid coaches in BR passenger service lasted in Scotland until early 1970 and after withdrawal from normal service in November 1969, No.1482 was incarcerated inside Bellahouston carriage cleaning shed. The coach was earmarked for preservation by the Scottish Railway Preservation Society, but it generously waived its option to purchase the carriage when the Bluebell Railway expressed an interest. The goodwill generated by this move no doubt hastened the

return to Scotland of the Bluebell's Caledonian Railway coach two years later. It may have been protected from the elements at Bellahouston, but No.1482 appears to have been attached to a steam heating boiler which rotted part of the floor, the replacement of which was a major job once the carriage arrived at the Bluebell. No.1482 is in service at the Bluebell at the time of writing in superb condition. This picture was taken in Scotland after the coach's final withdrawal from BR departmental service.

Author

Bulleid 'Multi-door' Coaches

The 'multi-door' 59ft-long 3-sets were used on various services in Sussex, and in this picture Ivatt-designed Class 2MT 2-6-2T No.41301 is depicted hauling a Horsham to Brighton train near Christ's Hospital on 10 March 1962. It should be noted that one third brake coach had been replaced by an unidentified Maunsell vehicle and the set number painted out.

John Beckett

Set Nos.963 to 980 (59ft. long)   **Coach Nos.S2841S to S2876S (Brake Third Corridor)**

Coach Nos.S5709S to S5726S (Composite Corridor)

Set Nos.981 to 984 (64ft. 6in. long)   **Coach Nos.S2877S to S2884S (Brake Third Corridor)** Not Illustrated

Coach Nos.S5727S to S5730S (Composite Corridor) Not Illustrated

In the late-1930s, shortly after Bulleid had taken over as the Southern Railway's Chief Mechanical Engineer, plans were laid for at least 150 new coaches for the Waterloo to Bournemouth and Weymouth services and, as the first part of this order, fifty-four 57ft. 11in. underframes were completed at Lancing works. The outbreak of hostilities put paid to any further carriage construction and it is thought that most of the underframes were stored in the Portsmouth area, though some were apparently used for the transportation of military equipment between Eastleigh and Lancing works and Southampton docks. In September 1944 instructions were issued for the construction of 22 three-coach sets (later amended to 18) and these entered traffic between November 1945 and April 1946. The sets consisted of two five-compartment third brake vehicles and a composite corridor carriage with four first class and three third class compartments. The former had very large brake vans which occupied just over a third of the length of the vehicle.

Externally the vehicles embodied many of the characteristics of Bulleid's electric stock, the continuous curve of the body profile from the floor to the roof, the butt-welded steel panelling and, of course, the distinctive lozenge-shaped toplight above the door droplights being noticeable features. Internally, however, the layout and décor perpetuated many of the design features from the Maunsell era. Perhaps it should be mentioned that, contrary to a common misconception, the bodies were built of wood (only the panels were steel) while the roofs were of traditional wood and canvas. The new sets were initially employed on Waterloo to West-of-England trains but were quickly displaced by later Bulleid stock which was considered more suitable for long distance services. They were then used on Waterloo to Bournemouth/Weymouth trains plus Salisbury workings and were later relegated to main-line stopping trains. Eleven of these sets was allocated to the Somerset and Dorset line in 1959, replacing Maunsell sets, while some migrated to the Central Section for Oxted line and Brighton-Horsham-Guildford services. These sets were hardly ever seen east of Tonbridge. Many of the sets were withdrawn *en masse* in December 1963 but a number of loose vehicles survived into 1967. In addition to the eighteen sets outlined above, there were four other multi-door sets constructed on the later 63ft. 5in. underframes in mid-1946. They were of very similar design, but the vehicles had an additional third class compartment with a corresponding increase in seating capacity. These sets were extremely elusive and no photographs of them were submitted for inclusion in this album. The composite corridor coaches were downgraded in 1964 and renumbered 1727-30 (as seconds), but retained their first class trimming until withdrawal. These composite coaches comprised the smallest fleet of the Bulleid production series of loco-hauled vehicles, a total of only four being constructed.

The uninitiated could easily mistake coach No.2849 as a Bulleid-designed electric multiple unit suburban vehicle which had an almost identical external appearance with bodyside doors to the compartments. This 59ft-long brake third was photographed at Bournemouth Central in the summer of 1967. The very large brake van will be noted. No.2849 was one of the few vehicles of this type that survived into 1967, when the last remaining examples were taken out of service.

Tim Robbins

Set No.653

Originating Company:	LSWR	**Type of Coach:**	Driving Brake Composite / Third
SR Diagram No:	417/33	**Build Date:**	1905 / 1899
Length:	46ft 6in / 58ft 0in	**Seating Capacity:**	1st - 13 / 3rd - 122

Undoubtedly, 2-coach set No.653, with its individual carriages out of all proportion to each other, is one of the strangest looking sets featured in this album. This picture was taken at Christ's Hospital station, just south of Horsham on the Mid Sussex line, and shows M7 Class locomotive No.30051 propelling a Horsham to Brighton train on 1 March 1959. The coach furthest away from the camera is a SECR ten-compartment third coach which is not part of set No.653. The vehicle at the front of the train is No.6429 which was built in 1905 as an 'emigrant' third (LSWR No.621 later Southern Railway 644). This nickname stemmed from the fact that the LSWR built a series of vehicles especially for use on trains conveying Eastern European emigrants who had landed in Great Britain at ports on the east coast, and were due to sail to America from west coast ports. These carriages were constructed to a composite loading gauge with very wide route availability, thus enabling them to travel over virtually any line in the country. The coaches had another unusual feature because they were built with an internal corridor, but no corridor connections on the vehicles' ends. The emigrant traffic fell away and by the mid-1920s No.6429 could be found ekeing out an existence on seasonal traffic, but its fortunes changed in 1935 when it was selected for conversion to a driving brake composite. It was fitted with a new underframe, supplied by BRCW Co., and extensively rebuilt for its new role with one compartment plus the toilet converted to a driving/guard/luggage compartment and two compartments at the opposite end upgraded to first class. The third class vehicle with which No.6429 was paired was No.2 which had been originally built as 50ft long tri-composite No.121 (later No.2305 and Southern Railway 4999) in December 1899 and was remounted on a standard 58ft. SR underframe in early 1935. An additional compartment was constructed, plus an expertly panelled-over 1ft. void which can be discerned between the fourth and fifth compartments in this shot. There were three other sets in this series and they could usually be found on the Central and South Eastern sections, though set No.652 worked the Bentley to Bordon branch for a while in the late 1940s: all had been withdrawn by the end of 1962.

Trevor Owen

Set No.652

Originating Company:	LSWR / SECR	**Type of Coach:**	Driving Brake Composite / Third
SR Diagram No:	417/52	**Build Dates:**	1905 / 1921
Length:	46ft 6in / 60ft 1in	**Seating Capacity:**	1st - 13 / 3rd - 132

Set No.652 is depicted near Ashurst, forming a Tunbridge Wells West to Oxted train, on 31 March 1962 with an unidentified SECR H Class 0-4-4T as motive power. This set was originally formed of two LSWR coaches, Nos.6428 and 1, but in 1958 the latter was exchanged for SECR ten-compartment third No.1074 which had been suitably converted for pull-push operation. Vehicle No.6428 started life as 'emigrant' third No.602 in 1905 and later became Southern Railway No.643. In 1935 it was withdrawn and underwent extensive modification (as coach No.6429, described previously), which included the fitting of a new underframe, to adapt it for pull-push operation and it emerged as No.6428. Coach No.1074 was built by the Birmingham Railway Carriage & Wagon Co. as No.1392 in August 1921 and soon afterwards became No.1074 under the Southern Railway numbering scheme. This set survived to become one of the very last 'vintage' pull-push sets in traffic, its official withdrawal date being 4 August 1962.

Trevor Owen

Set Nos.481 and 482

The 7.35am train to Allhallows, formed of set No.481, awaits departure from Grain on the sunny morning of 29 August 1959. Note the distinctive, modern signal box on the right of the shot.

Colour-Rail

Originating Company:	SECR	**Type of Coach:**	Driving Brake Third / Third
SR Diagram No:	223/364 (later 62)	**Build Date:**	1906
Length:	48ft 4in (both)	**Seating Capacity:**	1st - 15 (until October 1941) / 3rd - 88 (103 after October 1941)

Upon the grouping in 1923 the Southern Railway inherited eight SECR railmotors which were stored out of traffic with no prospect of future use. The coaches were built by the Metropolitan Amalgamated Railway Carriage & Wagon Company while the locomotive units were constructed by Kitson. Following an inspection it was decided that the engine units would be disposed of and the carriage portions converted into four two-coach sets. Two were earmarked for the Isle of Sheppey Light Railway and two (later set Nos.481 and 482) for pull-push operation on the Isle of Wight and they were ferried across to the Island in April 1925. The sets ran trials for a brief period over the Freshwater and Ventnor West lines but it appears that difficulties occurred and they were soon reallocated to Ryde for use on the Bembridge branch. In May 1927, however, the sets returned to the mainland for yet another period of storage. Full air control pull-push apparatus was fitted in 1930 and, presumably, this work included the incorporation of a standard pull-push driving end in the third class vehicles. Initially, they saw service on the Gravesend West Street branch, but in 1934 they were moved to the Dunton Green to Westerham branch where they stayed until almost the end of their lives. Ironically, this was where at least one of the vehicles had started its career twenty-eight years earlier! Just before its withdrawal from traffic set No.481 was put to work on the Gravesend Central to Allhallows/Grain branches, as seen in the accompanying illustrations.

SECR H Class 0-4-4T No.31512 gets under way from Gravesend Central with the 8.56am train to Allhallows on the same morning the previous shot was taken. Set No.481 was latterly comprised driving brake third No.3584 and third class coach No.914. The latter was formerly a composite coach, but it had been downgraded to third in October 1941.

Colour-Rail

A close-up view of the driving end of coach No.3583 at Dunton Green in the late 1950s. The figures on the white disc indicate the locomotive's duty number.

Colour-Rail

Set No.735

Originating Company:	LSWR	**Type of Coach:**	Driving Brake Third / Composite
SR Diagram No:	288/101	**Build Dates:**	1908 / 1907
Length:	46ft 6in	**Seating Capacity:**	1st - 12 / 3rd - 64

In 1943 it was decided to convert all of the surviving 'emigrant' coaches for pull-push operation, but this idea was not as straightforward as it might seem because the remaining eighteen 'emigrant' carriages were a limited assortment and many had to be extensively rebuilt in order to produce the required nine driving brake thirds and nine composite coaches. Coach No.4760, nearest to the camera, was originally built in 1908 as third No.1482 (later renumbered 90) and was further renumbered 654 when it became part of Southern Railway stock at the grouping. In 1935 a new underframe was fitted. In 1943 it was converted to pull-push operation and two compartments were upgraded to rather spartan first class and an outer corridor connection plus the lavatories were removed. In order to reflect the changes the coach was re-numbered again, this time to 4760. The driving third brake was built in June 1907 as third No.1443, later No.98, and was further renumbered by the Southern Railway, becoming their No.661. It was fitted with a new underframe in 1935. For conversion to pull-push operation in 1943 three compartments and a toilet were rebuilt as a guards, luggage and driving compartment, and one gangway and a second toilet were removed: the coach was re-numbered 2645. Set No.735 was originally allocated to the South Western section at Exeter for use on the Turnchapel and Callington branches and could also be found working to Exmouth, Sidmouth, Seaton or Yeovil. It could latterly be seen on the South Eastern section working to Allhallows, Gravesend West Street or Hawkhurst and final withdrawal came on 25 February 1961. Set No.735's extremely limited seating capacity, not to mention the corridor which enabled the guard to collect fares, made it ideal for use on the Allhallows branch, a little-used backwater destined for closure, and it is pictured at Allhallows station on 9 April 1960.

Rodney Lissenden

A further view of set No.735 at Allhallows, this time on 3 July 1960, a summer Sunday when the normal trains were strengthened, hence the four-coach formation. This photograph shows the corridor side of driving brake third vehicle No.2645. The photographer states that this set, together with set No.733, had earlier formed the 10.32am Gravesend Central to Allhallows train, this ensemble being hauled by brand new BRCW Type 3 No.D6511! The diesel locomotive was presumably running round when this picture was taken. One wonders how the passengers reacted to the sight of the locomotive crew travelling in style in a new diesel, while they had to suffer the indignity of riding in coaches constructed well before the First World War!   *John Langford*

Few illustrations used in this book were taken from bridges and, therefore, there is a scarcity of pictures where a coach's roof can clearly be seen. The roofs of the vehicles in set No.735 stand out in this shot which was taken from the station footbridge at Graves-end Central during the summer of 1960. Note that the coaches have different roof ventilators, but at least the rain strips and (what appear to be) destination board brackets seem to be the same on both vehicles. The rest of the picture exudes the atmosphere of the railway at that time, with coal wagons in the goods yard, accompanied by a spare coach, a large green running-in board, a platform barrow and colourful array of posters. Marvellous!   *Barry Blacklock / Roy Denison collection*

Set No.659

Originating Company:	SECR	**Type of Coach:**	Driving Brake Composite / Third
SR Diagram No:	429/155	**Build Dates:**	1909 (both vehicles)
Length:	50ft 1in / 54ft 1in	**Seating Capacity:**	1st - 14 / 3rd - 98

Set No.659 was formed as a direct consequence of the Swanley Junction accident on 27 July 1937 in which 'Birdcage' set No.535 was involved. One of the brake coaches was a write-off, while the intermediate composite vehicle was badly damaged. The remaining brake carriage survived the incident practically unscathed. The last-mentioned vehicle, No.3324, was used, together with the composite coach, No.5418, which was rebuilt as a driving composite brake, to form pull-push set No.659 from April 1938. The composite vehicle was renumbered 6409 and this was the first pull-push set formed entirely of ordinary SECR coaches. This set was unique in that vehicle No.3324 retained its 'Birdcage' lookout, and that coach had a particular claim to fame because it eventually became the last 'Birdcage' coach in traffic on BR, running until late 1961. The set was initially employed on the Yeovil Junction to Yeovil Town shuttle where its two brake vans were especially useful for conveying the large amount of mail and luggage being transferred on and off main line trains. In October 1948 the set returned to its home territory, being recorded at Hawkhurst, Maidstone, Tonbridge and Westerham. Its career came to an end in November 1961 by which time it was merely a 'stand by' set in case of any shortages. It was photographed at Tunbridge Wells West in October 1961.

Roy Hobbs

Set No.373

In February 1906 three motor trains were introduced by the LSWR for use on local services in the Plymouth district, each consisting of a saloon third plus a saloon brake third powered initially by diminutive C14 Class 2-2-0Ts. Three years later a three-car set, which included two brake composite vehicles, was built for use on the Weymouth to Portland and Easton branch, the design closely resembling that of the earlier sets. Three more pull-push sets (later SR Nos.372-374) were ordered in June 1913 for use on the Seaton plus

Lee-on-the-Solent branches and local workings in the Exeter area. These sets were provided at first with gas lighting but this was converted to electricity in 1919/20 and further modifications in 1929/30 entailed the removal of the LSWR cable system and the fitting of air control apparatus and standard SR driving ends. By far the most unusual design feature of these sets were the fabricated metal gates which gave the sets an extremely distinctive appearance and resulted in them being universally known as the 'gate' stock. Set No.373, seen here on (what appears to be) a Yeovil Junction-Yeovil Town train in the late 1950s, was at one time allocated to the Seaton branch but for many years was associated with local services in the Plymouth area. Towards the end of its career the set was in great demand for rail tours. In July 1960 Set No.373 was paired with LSWR Beattie well tank locomotive No.30587 during centenary celebrations at Exeter Central and there was speculation that it might be preserved. Alas, it suffered water damage while stored at Crediton and the vehicles were scrapped in November 1960 - a sad loss. It should be noted that by the time of this picture many of the bodyside mouldings had been covered by steel sheeting.

R.C. Riley

Originating Company:	LSWR	**Type of Coach:**	Driving Brake Third / Third
SR Diagram No:	414/27	**Build Date:**	1914
Length:	56ft 0in (both)	**Seating Capacity:**	2nd - 129 (from August 1939 when 1st class downgraded)

A shot of coach No.2622 at Seaton Junction on 14 May 1960, showing part of a 'gate' which gave these sets their nickname. The angle of the sun is striking some of the internal partitions, thus giving a hint of what the interior of this distinctive set was like.

John Langford

Originating Company:	SECR/LBSCR	Type of Coach:	Driving Brake Composite / Third
SR Diagram No:	421/80	Build Dates:	1916 / 1919
Length:	60ft 1in / 54ft 0in	Seating Capacity:	1st - 13 / 3rd - 125

This set was a hybrid and originally formed in 1941 using a LSWR third plus a former SECR steel-panelled brake converted to a driving brake composite. The former vehicle started life in November 1907 as composite No.279, but was later downgraded and numbered 608 in the Southern Railway series. It was fitted with pull-push equipment in August 1941 for use in set No.37. The SECR coach entered service in July 1916 as second/third class composite brake No.1342 and later became No.3539. Like its companion vehicle, it was modified for pull-push operation in 1941 and was renumbered 6410. A driving end was added to the brake compartment, the toilets were sealed out of use and the two former second class compartments were upgraded to first class. This set was nominally allocated for use in Hampshire, but in reality it was based at either Horsham or Tunbridge Wells West, its duties taking it to Guildford, Brighton, Tonbridge or Oxted. In 1954 the LSWR trailer was withdrawn and replaced by LBSCR 'luggage third' No.2193 of 1919 vintage which had previously been formed in set No.759. This coach had been built in December 1919 as a driving trailer composite for the AC electrification, No.4110 to diagram 285. It did not see electric service and was used as a steam-hauled composite, later Southern Railway No.6268, with the intended driving compartment used as a luggage locker. In 1932, as it was not required for conversion to DC stock, it was reduced to all third, air control was fitted and it was allocated to set No.759 to replace a condemned vehicle. The new diagram number was 80 and the luggage locker was retained. Set No.759 was withdrawn in 1954 and coach No.2193 was re-allocated. Set No.37 continued to operate from Horsham but was moved to the South Eastern Section in late 1959, where it ended its days on services radiating from Tonbridge and Maidstone West. Set No.37, which is seen here at Sevenoaks on 17 April 1960, was withdrawn in December 1960.

Colour-Rail

Set No.656

A train formed of two-coach set No.656, sits at Hawkhurst station's platform after arrival from Paddock Wood on 13 April 1961, just a couple of months before services ceased. This set has a special claim to fame because it was the last pull-push set created from pre-grouping SECR stock. It was formed in 1956 from third brake coach No.3542 and composite No.5499 both of which had previously been part of set No.633; this set was disbanded and vehicle No.3470, the set's other third brake, was withdrawn from traffic.

Vehicle Nos.3542 and 5499 had originally been constructed as SECR Nos.1350 and 1349 respectively at Ashford works in October 1917. Set No.656 made its first appearance in traffic at the start of the summer 1957 timetable and was always based on the Central or South Eastern sections. Towards the end of its short career it appeared regularly on the Oxted to Tunbridge Wells West service until withdrawn in January 1962.

Colour-Rail

Originating Company:	SECR	**Type of Coach:**	Driving Brake Third / Composite
SR Diagram No:	162A/316A	**Build Date:**	1917
Length:	60ft 1in	**Seating Capacity:**	1st - 20 / 3rd - 104

A further view of set No.656, this time taken at Tonbridge on 17 April 1960, with coach No.5499 nearest to the camera. This coach featured a first class saloon with a large window and had very comfortable armchairs, the backs of which can just be discerned. There were two lavatories, one serving the aforementioned saloon, while the other was provided for passengers in the adjacent former first class compartment, which is the second compartment from the right in the photograph. There remains another first class compartment on the other side of the saloon while the three compartments furthest away from the camera were former second class, later thirds (now classified 'second' by the date of this picture). Strangely, neither of the two first class compartments nearest to the photographer seem to have appropriate markings, so perhaps they had been downgraded by this date. The set was photographed against the background of Tonbridge marshalling yard which is full of vans and wagons of all shapes and sizes - one wonders what happened to all of that railborne traffic.

Colour-Rail

Set No.716

Originating Company:	LBSCR	**Type of Coach:**	Driving Brake Third / Composite
SR Diagram No:	193/350	**Build Date:**	1921
Length:	56ft 0in (both)	**Seating Capacity:**	1st - 25 / 3rd - 104

There was a lull in coaching stock construction during the First World War but in 1921 four more 2-coach sets were authorised by the LBSCR, later Nos.981 to 984. The set depicted was formerly No.983 and was renumbered 716 in 1937. It consisted of driving third brake No.1403 and composite trailer No.647 which were renumbered 3848 and 6239 respectively at the Grouping. These sets had four first class compartments and therefore offered a greater proportion of first class accommodation than any other LBSCR pull-push set. Set No.716 was initially allocated to Eastbourne for use on the services to Hastings and Rye, but by the 1930s could be seen on the New Romney and Hythe branches. It later saw use on the Crowhurst to Bexhill West branch and lasted in traffic until 8 October 1960. This photograph shows the set forming part of a Gravesend Central to Allhallows train on 3 August 1959, accompanied by former SECR railmotor set No.481. An unidentified train, apparently formed of a selection of 'Southern' coaches, stands on the up through line adding interest to the scene. One wonders what fascinating vehicles may have been in that train's formation!

John Langford

Set No.1

Originating Company:	LSWR/SECR	Type of Coach:	Driving Brake Composite / Third
SR Diagram No:	419/52	Build Dates:	1911 / 1921
Length:	56ft 0in / 60ft 1in	Seating Capacity:	1st - 10 / 3rd - 138

This set was originally formed in 1937 with a suitably converted 56ft.-long brake composite, No.6488 (previously LSWR No.1024), and rebuilt 58ft. (ex composite) brake third coach No.2620. Unusually, this set used to have brake vans in both vehicles but in July 1958 No.2620 was replaced by a former SECR ten compartment third No.1066. This set was photographed at Borden while forming a Railway Enthusiasts Club rail tour on 15 October 1960. M7 class 0-4-4T No.30028 was providing the motive power. The driving brake composite coach incorporated no fewer than four lavatory compartments, two of which served first class passengers while the other two were for the use of those in the third class. Incredibly, despite this gross over provision most of the third class passengers still did not have access to a toilet. This set spent its entire career on the South Western Section.

Trevor Owen

Set Nos.383 and 384

Originating Company:	LSWR	**Type of Coach:**	Driving Brake Third / Brake Composite
SR Diagram No:	136/414	**Build Date:**	1925
Length:	57ft 0in	**Seating Capacity:**	1st - 12 / 3rd - 100

This set was formed in 1925 of 'Ironclad' carriages for use on through services from Waterloo to Lymington Pier, Swanage and the west of England. When it first entered service set No.383 doubtless ventured along the Swanage branch regularly and, by a remarkable twist of fate following its replacement in the late 1940s by newly-built Bulleid vehicles, it ended its days on the Swanage branch on purely local services almost forty years later. This photograph was taken at Wareham on 13 May 1962 and depicts set No.383, plus a strengthening coach, standing in the down platform as a large crowd of passengers wait on the opposite platform for an eastbound train. The driving brake third coach, nearest to the camera, comprised of seven compartments each seating eight passengers, plus a coupe at the inner end of the vehicle seating a further six. The trailer brake composite had four third class compartments and two first class in the middle of the vehicle; once again there was a coupe seating a further six third class passengers. The coming of the Bulleid two-coach sets in 1946-48 meant that the 'Ironclads' were redundant and it was decided to convert them for pull-push operation. For conversion the gangway connections were removed, the toilets abolished and the space converted into a coupe compartment. An additional third class compartment was created in part of the van space of the third brake, the van end of the brake third being converted to the standard pull-push format. Five 'Ironclad' brake third/brake composite sets were converted, four between October 1948 and September 1949 as the sets became due for shops. Conversion of set No.385 followed in March 1952. Some of the sets were repainted in malachite green and others BR crimson lake. Set No.383 was based at Yeovil for a long time and then worked on the Swanage branch, as seen here. Apart from the late-1950s Maunsell sets, these 'Ironclad' sets lasted longer than almost any other SR pull-push stock and most survived until the end of December 1962.

Colour-Rail

How different the 'Ironclad' sets looked in BR crimson lake livery! Set No.384 worked the Bentley to Bordon branch for some years and when that branch was closed it was transferred to Bournemouth for use on the 'Old Road' from there to Brockenhurst via Wimborne or the Lymington branch. It was photographed at Brockenhurst in September 1960, accompanied by M7 Class No.30480.

Colour-Rail

Photographed on 9 September 1962, just a few months away from withdrawal, set No.383 looks extremely smart as it forms the 4.45pm Wareham to Swanage train with M7 Class 0-4-4T No.30111 as motive power. This scene was recorded as the train approached Corfe Castle station; the strengthening coach appears to be No.1050, the history of which is detailed elsewhere in this album.

John Beckett

Set Nos.601 to 620

Originating Company:	SR	**Type of Coach:**	Driving Brake Composite Corridor / Open Second Corridor
SR Diagram No:	2407/2023	**Build Dates:**	1935 / 1933
Length:	59ft 0in	**Seating Capacity:**	1st - 12 / 2nd - 88

In the late 1950s there were forty-six vintage pull-push sets still in daily use on the SR and doubts were expressed about their safety, especially their crash-worthiness and the likelihood of them catching fire due to electrical arcing if involved in an accident in the third rail area. In addition, in 1959 the British Transport Commission decreed, in effect, that any carriage more than thirty years old should be consigned to the scrap heap and this brought matters to a head. There was no immediate prospect of replacement diesel units nor electrification and, of course, the notorious Beeching Plan was still some way off, so the Southern Region decided to create twenty 'new' pull-push sets using more modern existing steam coaches, the vehicle types being Maunsell composite brakes and open seconds that were constructed in 1935 and 1933 respectively. The end corridor connections were removed and large electric unit type buffers fitted, but the intermediate gangways were retained to facilitate fare collection by the guard. Part of the brake area of the composite coach was converted into a driver's cab and two modestly-sized end windows were provided plus side droplights. The sets were introduced gradually between October 1959 and February 1961, with the result that by early 1962 only a handful of the older sets remained at work, at either Bournemouth or Tunbridge Wells West. Initially, the newly-formed sets were allocated to specific areas but subsequently this was largely abandoned and sets were moved around the region. In this view set No.610, in immaculate condition, is seen forming a Railway Enthusiasts Club rail tour at Sharnal Street on 24 September 1960. The set's excellent condition is explained by the fact that it had only been released to traffic two months previously! This set was based at Yeovil for a time and was on the 'wrong' side of the regional border when the Western Region took over the tracks west of Salisbury in January 1963: however, it subsequently returned to the SR. Line closures and the coming of the diesel units ensured that these sets were short-lived and, indeed, set No.607 only lasted from January 1960 to September 1961, being disbanded as a result of an accident at Eastbourne. General withdrawal of the sets commenced in December 1963, their last stronghold being the Bournemouth area where they worked the Swanage and Lymington branches plus the service to Brockenhurst via Wimborne. Withdrawal of the last motor-fitted LSWR M7 Class 0-4-4Ts in May 1964 brought nearly sixty years of pull-push operation on the 'Southern' to an end, but some sets remained available for traffic for a few more months but not, of course, in pull-push mode.

Trevor Owen

The final outposts of pull-push working on the 'Southern' were, as previously mentioned, Bournemouth and Tunbridge Wells West and in this view, taken on 11 November 1961, an unidentified SECR H Class 0-4-4T propels a Tunbridge Wells West to Oxted train, formed of set No.601, away from its Groombridge station stop. In contrast to the previous illustration, this photograph shows the compartment side of the driving brake composite coach. It is sad to reflect that at one time the section of line between here and Tunbridge Wells, onto which services from Brighton, Eastbourne, Oxted and Three Bridges converged, had a very frequent service but now sees no passenger services at all apart from those of the preserved Spa Valley Railway.

John Beckett

Photographed in the final year of pull-push operation on the Southern Region, M7 Class 0-4-4T No.30111 hauls an unidentified up three-coach working, possibly at Lymington Junction west of Brockenhurst. The two coaches at the rear of the train comprise set No.613, this being one of the very few Maunsell sets to sport a yellow stripe at cantrail level denoting first class accommodation. The strengthening carriage immediately behind the engine is a Maunsell open second, probably a spare coach from a pull-push set.

Colour-Rail

Set No.721

Originating Company:	LBSCR	**Type of Coach:**	Driving Brake Third / Composite
SR Diagram No:	194/351	**Build Date:**	1922
Length:	54ft 0in (both)	**Seating Capacity:**	1st - 13 / 3rd - 104

In this gem of a photograph taken at Godalming goods depot on 5 October 1957, the Railway Enthusiasts Club's 'The Compass Rose' rail tour is seen pausing with LSWR M7 Class 0-4-4T No.30051 in charge. The recently out-shopped pull-push set, in sparkling crimson lake livery, forming the train is No.721 which consisted of driving brake third No.3853 (nearest to the camera) and trailer composite No.6248. This set was constructed in 1922 as No.988 and was among the last pull-push sets authorised for construction by the LBSCR, in this case for general branch line use without any specific allocation. Carriage No.3853 was built as No.1408 and offered 48 third class seats while its accompanying composite coach, originally No.656, had 13 first class and 56 third class seats. Despite being not given an 'official' allocation when built the set was usually found at Littlehampton during the 1930s, while in 1945 its allocation was given as the Central Section. The set's number was changed to 721 in 1937. Both vehicles had open sided compartments, but at least the two first class compartments had a degree of privacy provided by sliding doors separating them both from the third class accommodation and from each other. Despite obviously having been through works not long before this picture was taken, the set was withdrawn on 17 May 1958 - what a waste!

Trevor Owen

Set No.446

Originating Company:	SR	**Type of Coach:**	Brake Third Corridor / Composite Corridor / Brake Third Corridor
SR Diagram No:	2101/2301/2101	**Build Date:**	1928
Length:	59ft 0in	**Seating Capacity:**	1st - 24 / 3rd - 88

This picture depicts LMSR 2P Class 4-4-0 No.40698 leaving Broadstone in charge of a Bath to Bournemouth passenger working on 4 July 1959. The tracks on the left lead to Hamworthy Junction. The train's formation comprises Maunsell 3-set No.446 plus an unidentified vehicle on the rear. The 3-set was one of four identical sets (Nos.445 to 448) ordered in 1926 for services from London to Plymouth, Torrington plus Ilfracombe, and this particular set was formed of vehicle Nos.4057, 5148 and 4058; it entered traffic in August 1928. It is generally believed that this small batch of three coach sets was built by the Metropolitan Carriage, Wagon & Finance Co., but the official coaching stock registers indicate that the sets were constructed by the Southern Railway. These sets, which were almost identical to ten three coach sets built in 1926, were notable because of their very low seating capacity, this disadvantage being balanced by their extra large brake vans that were no doubt appreciated by holiday-makers taking huge amounts of luggage on holiday. Another unusual characteristic of these sets was the brake vehicles' half curved, half straight bodyside profile, the long straight, narrow section being due to the fact that guards' lookouts were provided. Note also the uniform height of the windows which was a design feature of all coaches built between 1926 and mid-1929. Towards the end of their lives these sets were allocated to the Somerset & Dorset line, set No.446 eventually being withdrawn from traffic on 1 April 1961.

Trevor Owen

Set No.189

Originating Company:	SR	**Type of Coach:**	Brake Third Corridor / Composite Corridor
SR Diagram No:	2104/2302	**Build Date:**	1931
Length:	59ft 0in	**Seating Capacity:**	1st - 32 / 3rd - 144

A superb cloud formation, brilliant afternoon sunshine and vivid autumn tints; this was the scene at Eridge on 29 October 1961 as the 12.45pm Eastbourne to Tunbridge Wells West train, hauled by BR Standard Class 4MT No.80031, waits in the up loop. The coaches forming the train comprise recently *ex*-works four-coach Maunsell set No.189 of 1931 vintage. Note that the sun is highlighting the cream-painted compartment partition panels in the coach nearest to the camera. This set was originally built for London Victoria to Eastbourne and Hastings services and was made up of two corridor composite coaches plus two brake third corridor vehicles, the formation being clearly visible in the picture. In 1962 it was decided to split all of the remaining four-coach Maunsell sets into two 2-coach sets, vehicle Nos.3705 and 5619 from set No.189 becoming set No.447 whilst coach Nos.3704 and 5618 retained their original set number. These sets apparently survived on the Reading to Tonbridge service until early 1965, thus becoming some of the last Maunsell era carriages in BR passenger service.

John Langford

Coach No.S2454

Originating Company:	SECR	**Type of Coach:**	Lavatory Composite Brake	
SR Diagram No:	158	**Build Date:**	1910	
Length:	54ft 1in	**Seating Capacity:**	2nd - 7 / 3rd - 48	

This coach started its career in December 1910 at Ashford works as SECR lavatory brake composite carriage No.1101 and originally had five third class and one second class compartment plus two lavatories. One toilet was provided for the sole use of the passengers travelling in the second class accommodation while the other served (a maximum of eight!) passengers in the adjacent third class compartment. The remaining forty third class passengers did not have access to a toilet. When the Southern Railway came into being the coach was renumbered 3369. In April 1949 it was taken into Lancing works for drastic surgery prior to a future role on the Isle of Wight, the 'birdcage' brake compartment being converted into two new third class passenger compartments. The two lavatories were also stripped out, becoming a five-seat coupe compartment accessed from the adjacent former second class compartment, which is at the far end of the vehicle in this photograph. The much-altered carriage was shipped to the island in May 1949 and its career ended when it was scrapped at Newport in November 1966, following withdrawal on 22 October. The position of the former 'birdcage' brake (note the different style of panelling) can be clearly seen in this picture which was taken at Newport on 9 August 1965. The location of the coupe compartment is indicated by the 'odd' droplight at the far end of the vehicle. The other coach in the picture appears to be of an identical type.

Colour-Rail

Coach No.S2438

Originating Company:	SECR	**Type of Coach:**	Third
SR Diagram No:	158	**Build Date:**	1910
Length:	54ft 1in	**Seating Capacity:**	3rd - 83

This coach shares a similar history to No.2454. It was originally SECR No.1097 and became No.3365 upon the Grouping in 1923. It was withdrawn from mainland service in April 1948 and converted for use on the Isle of Wight, being one of eighteen vehicles shipped to the island in 1948/49. It lasted in traffic on the island until October 1966. Line closures in the 1950s rendered many of this batch of coaches redundant, but some survived until the final year of steam in 1966. This picture, which was taken at Cowes on 19 September 1964, shows the former second class end of the vehicle with a coupe compartment where the lavatories used to be located.

Colour-Rail

Coach No.S1015

Originating Company:	SECR	**Type of Coach:**	Full brake (originally Composite Brake)
SR Diagram No:	891	**Build Date:**	1911
Length:	54ft 1in	**Seating Capacity:**	

This vehicle began life as SECR 'Birdcage' brake coach No.1144 at Ashford works in December 1911 and originally had six third class compartments plus one second class and was allocated to set No.105. In theory it became number 3398 after the Grouping in set No.544, but the actual physical renumbering was apparently not carried out until September 1926. The coach was withdrawn from mainland service on 17 April 1948, but earmarked for use on the Isle of Wight (as No.4140) and underwent extensive modification prior to movement to the island. Three compartments were removed in order to provide additional luggage capacity and an extra set of double doors was fitted, the 'new', enlarged brake van occupying just over half of the vehicle's length. Despite these changes, passengers who occupied the former second class compartment at the end of the carriage had the benefit of more space, albeit an extra width of six inches! In 1956 coach No.4140 was one of four selected for further conversion to a full brake and in the process it lost much of its character, the bodywork being encased in steel sheeting. The guard's position at one end of the vehicle was retained together with the end look out windows introduced for use in the Isle of Wight. It was renumbered yet again, becoming No.1015, and this interesting carriage is seen here at Newport on the site of the engine shed on 9 August 1965. It was finally withdrawn on 19 November 1966.

Colour-Rail

Coach No.S6986 formerly No.57

Originating Company:	LBSCR	**Type of Coach:**	Invalid or Family Saloon
SR Diagram No:	645	**Build Date:**	1916
Length:	54ft 0in	**Seating Capacity:**	1st - 12 / 3rd - 36 (after conversion for use on Isle of Wight)

This coach is depicted at Merstone Junction on an unknown date in the 1950s. This unique vehicle has an especially interesting history, being built in 1916 as an invalid or family saloon; it was constructed with gangways at both ends. The carriage had no specific workings. In 1934 (by this time it had been renumbered 7973) it was converted to a composite brake for use on the Isle of Wight and its gangways were removed but the lavatory was retained and it achieved a degree of fame because it was the only coach on the island with this operational facility. It was renumbered once more, becoming No.6986 in the I.O.W. number series. The coach was used for some years on 'The Tourist', the island's only named train which operated from Ventnor to Freshwater via Sandown, but when the Freshwater line was closed in 1953 No.6986 was, in effect, redundant and was withdrawn as a passenger-carrying vehicle on 2 June 1956. Its career was far from over, however, and in 1959 it was converted at Ryde works to a tool van for use with the Ryde motive power department breakdown crane, its official date of conversion being 29 August 1959, from which date it was known as DS70008. Regrettably, after a particularly interesting life, No.DS70008 was withdrawn on 1 April 1967 and subsequently cut-up for scrap. It is believed to have been the last LBSCR coach scrapped by BR.

Colour-Rail

Coach No.DS70008 formerly No.S6986

DS70008 is seen at Ryde St. John's Road motive power depot on 27 September 1959, looking absolutely splendid in crimson livery following conversion to a service vehicle. Ryde works was justly famed for the extremely high standard of its work to which the paint finish of this vehicle bears ample testament.

Colour-Rail

Coach No.S4159

Originating Company:	LBSCR	**Type of Coach:**	Third Brake
SR Diagram No:	204	**Build Date:**	1912
Length:	54ft 0in	**Seating Capacity:**	3rd - 70

This coach was one of the few seven compartment third brake vehicles built, and was constructed at Lancing as LBSCR No.105, its official 'build date' being June 1912. It became Southern Railway number 4038 in 1924 and was shipped to the Isle of Wight in May 1936, being renumbered 4159 in the island's brake third series. In the post war years these vehicles tended to be used on the Ryde to Cowes route where their relatively high number of seats compensated for the lower seating capacity of other coaches used on the Cowes line. Following the closure of that route in February 1966 No.4159 was used on the Ryde to Shanklin line, surviving until the end of the summer timetable. Its official withdrawal date was 24 September 1966 and the vehicle was broken up at Newport a few months later. No.4159 is depicted at Newport on 12 August 1965 and appears to be in pristine condition following an overhaul. It is sad to think that it lasted in traffic for only another year after this photograph was taken - what a shame!

David Wigley

Coach No.S4154

Originating Company:	SBSCR	**Type of Coach:**	Brake Third
SR Diagram No:	203	**Build Date:**	1916
Length:	54ft 0in	**Seating Capacity:**	3rd - 60

A lovely portrait of vehicle No.4154, looking very smart in crimson livery, posing for its photograph in the sun at Ryde St. John's Road on 25 June 1957. This coach first saw the light of day in June 1916 and was originally numbered 649 in the LBSCR series. When the LBSCR was absorbed by the Southern Railway in 1923 it was renumbered 4027. In May 1936 it was transferred to the Isle of Wight and was renumbered yet again, becoming 4154 in the island series and was one of ten similar coaches allocated to the island. Six other carriages of this type had their brake vans abolished and were converted to nine compartment coaches for use on the island. No.4154 survived in service until February 1966, being withdrawn following the cessation of passenger services on the Ryde to Cowes line.

R.C. Riley

Coach No.S4168

Originating Company:	LBSCR	**Type of Coach:**	Brake Third
SR Diagram No:	137	**Build Date:**	1922
Length:	54ft 0in	**Seating Capacity:**	3rd - 50

Constructed at Lancing works in June 1922 on an earlier 'Balloon' coach's underframe, vehicle No.4168 was originally Southern Railway number 3870 and did not carry No.4168 until its transfer to the Isle of Wight in April 1938. Initially, it worked on the Bembridge branch and later could be seen on more general duties on the island. It was often merely a 'spare' coach and could be observed berthed at Newport. No.4168 really came into its own in the winter of 1966 when Ryde Pier Head station was closed in connection with alterations for the electric services that were due to start in 1967. Mails and parcels had to be handled at Ryde Esplanade station, a less than ideal location, and to facilitate their easy transfer a 3-coach train was formed which included SECR and LBSCR brake coaches back to back. Needless to say, the LBSCR carriage selected for these duties was No.4168 which had the advantage of a huge brake area - just the job! No.4168, therefore, lasted until the end of steam traction on the island, its official withdrawal date being 14 January 1967. It should be noted that from the end of the Second World War until the cessation of steam working, No.4168 had a claim to fame as the only five-compartment LBSCR coach in service on the island. It is now preserved on the Isle of Wight Steam Railway. The coach was photographed at Newport on 22 August 1965.

Colour-Rail

Inspection Saloon Coach No.DS1

Originating Company:	LSWR	Type of Coach:	Director's Saloon
SR Diagram No:	Not known	Build Date:	1885
Length:	46ft 0in	Seating Capacity:	18

Built in 1885 at a cost of £1,261.8s.11d., this coach was not numbered until 1895 when it became No.21S and was later known as Inspection Coach No.1. The Southern Railway recorded it on its list of service vehicles as No.1S and in BR days it was known as No. DS1. It is seen here at Faversham on 20 September 1959: the vehicle was a regular sight on the South Eastern Division in the late 1950s/early 1960s in connection with drivers' route learning for the Kent Coast Electrification. The accommodation consisted originally of a kitchen and lavatory towards the middle of the coach, while there were also three separate seating areas with some plush armchairs. The carriage was gas lit when built but had been converted to electric lighting by 1925. The vehicle was particularly noteworthy because of its domed ends, a very unusual feature and certainly one not found on other LSWR coaches. In days gone by the carriage also had two raised sections of the roof, rather similar to clerestories, but these were later removed. During June 1950 the body of No.DS1 was lifted from its original underframe and mounted on a shortened underframe from 1910-built LSWR composite coach No.5097. The vehicle was repainted in BR lined crimson at this time, but it could be said that the lining above the windows looked messy and was a totally unnecessary embellishment. Gas tanks for the kitchen appliances were fitted on the roof for a time but these were removed in April 1958. In November 1962 No.DS1 was replaced by No.DS70155, which had been converted from a Maunsell coach, and it was withdrawn from service after a very long life on 28 April 1963.

R.C. Riley

Coach No.S7919S

Originating Company:	SECR	**Type of Coach:**	First Saloon Lavatory
SR Diagram No:	618	**Build Date:**	1905
Length:	50ft 1in	**Seating Capacity:**	1st - 22

This vehicle was one of three similar carriages ordered from the Metropolitan Amalgamated Railway Carriage & Wagon Co. in August 1904 and delivered during the following year. No.7919 is depicted at Eardley Road sidings on 30 October 1960. All the vehicles were built to the same basic dimensions but had considerable detail differences. No.7919 was constructed as SECR No.3785 and had teak body framing with mahogany panels. The underframe was of oak with steel bolsters and longitudinals. When built No.7919 had a symmetrical layout with a centrally positioned 20ft. long central saloon with a small compartment and lavatory at each end of the coach. Gangway connections were fitted at each end. No.7919 entered traffic in April 1905 and was marshalled in the Royal train which at that time apparently comprised a maximum of seven vehicles. In March 1937 the SR Board authorised the conversion of No.7919 into an invalid saloon, and a bed, armchairs and table were placed in the main saloon and a luggage compartment was installed, access to this being through sets of double doors on each side of the coach. A separate set of double doors on each side provided access to the main saloon. No.7919 lasted in this guise for many years and was eventually withdrawn in September 1959 when it was replaced by converted SR carriages.

R.C. Riley

Coach No.AD3321 formerly LSWR No.4132

Originating Company:	LSWR	**Type of Coach:**	Kitchen Dining Saloon (later Nondescript Saloon)
SR Diagram No:	593 (after conversion)	**Build Date:**	1907
Length:	56ft 0in	**Seating Capacity:**	40 (as picnic saloon)

This photograph of coach No.AD3321 was taken at Craven Hill, on the Bicester Military Railway, on 23 September 1972. This vehicle was constructed by the LSWR, which allotted the number No.70, and the coach was completed in May 1907. It was renumbered 4132 in July 1919 and later became No.7832 under the Southern Railway regime. It was originally built with a clerestory roof but this was removed in 1931 when the carriage was converted to a nondescript saloon. It was withdrawn from ordinary traffic on 6 October 1943 and found a further lease of life in army service as ambulance car No.1641 at the Longmoor Military Railway prior to removal to Bicester. It was subsequently converted to a cinema coach on an unknown date. It is preserved at the time of writing on the Pontypool and Blaenavon Railway.

David Wigley

Coach No.WD3007

Originating Company:	LSWR	**Type of Coach:**	Inspection Saloon
SR Diagram No:	581	**Build Date:**	1910
Length:	46ft 6in	**Seating Capacity:**	1st - 11 / 3rd - 5

Photographed on a day when there was a visiting rail tour from London (hence the BR Standard Mk.1 coaches just visible in the background) LSWR inspection Saloon No.3007 is seen at Longmoor Downs, on the Longmoor Military Railway, on 30 April 1966. No.3007 was built at Eastleigh in November 1910 as invalid saloon No.11, being renumbered 4105 from 1912. After the grouping it became No.7803 and was eventually sold to the army in 1938. When built it was fitted with end corridor connections and the former position of these is indicated by the relatively new panelling. After the closure of the army railway system at Longmoor the saloon went to the Severn Valley Line, but No.3007 later returned nearer home, so to speak, and is now in the care of the Kent & East Sussex Railway.

Roy Hobbs

Coach No.S291S formerly LBSCR No.60

Originating Company:	LBSCR	**Type of Coach:**	Director's Saloon
SR Diagram No:	Not known	**Build Date:**	1914
Length:	63ft 8in	**Seating Capacity:**	28 Un-classed

The former LBSCR directors' inspection saloon, No.DS291, is seen at Stewarts Lane depot on 26 May 1958. This magnificent vehicle is one of the most opulent, probably *the* most opulent, featured in this album. It was constructed at Lancing works in 1914 to the design of A.H. Panter, LBSCR Carriage & Wagon Superintendent, for the use of the directors and principal officers of that company. It is divided into two main compartments (usually referred to as observatories) twenty-six and twelve feet long respectively which are connected by a side corridor. The corridor also gives access to a butler's pantry (in effect a small kitchen area) and a lavatory. The coach is bow ended and was originally fitted with three large windows at each end to provide the occupants with an uninterrupted view of the track when running out on the line. The internal panelling is of mahogany and satin wood and the particularly ornate ceilings are of a delicate 'Adams' design. The coach is mounted on two six-wheeled bogies. When new the vehicle was painted in standard LBSCR umber brown livery with gold lining, the roof being painted white. One wonders how the white roof was kept looking pristine in the steam era! The LBSCR coat-of-arms adorned each side of the coach together with the vehicle's number. After the grouping in 1923 the Southern Railway renumbered the carriage 291S and repainted it in their own dark green livery. Several structural alterations were also made, perhaps the most noticeable being the fitting of sliding toplights and smaller sidelights in place of the large, one-piece sidelights originally fitted. A handbrake, which is clearly visible in the picture, was apparently fitted at the same time. In December 1933 glazed gangway doors were installed and subsequently gangways were fitted, these being somewhat shorter than ordinary gangways due the coach being bow-ended. In early BR days it was repainted in crimson and cream livery and remained in these colours until November 1962 when it was repainted in SR green livery: dual heating (electric heating in addition to the normal steam heating) was fitted at this time. It remained in service as an inspection saloon until withdrawn in 1964 and its preservation by BR's Curator of Historical Relics was mooted, but this later proved impracticable and the Bluebell Railway stepped in to acquire this historic vehicle, which was (at that time) the last LBSCR coach on the mainland. The coach arrived at Sheffield Park on 4 August 1965 and was used on Bluebell trains, usually on special occasions, during the late 1960s and early 1970s. Sadly, it has not appeared in public service for many years and because it is not suitable for everyday use due to its very low seating capacity, not to mention the extensive and expensive restoration work required, its repair appears to be low on the railway's priorities.

R.C. Riley

Coach No.DS70155 formerly SR No.5600

Originating Company:	SR (rebuilt 1962)	**Type of Coach:**	Inspection Saloon
SR Diagram No:	1958	**Build Date:**	1931
Length:	59ft 0in	**Seating Capacity:**	18 plus 9 unclassed (for officers)

The Inspection Saloon seen here was originally Hastings Line corridor composite coach No.5600, which was withdrawn from traffic in August 1959, and the saloon was used mainly for drivers' route learning training. It was rebuilt at Eastleigh and emerged from the works in November 1962. The accommodation included an eighteen-seat saloon at one end and a nine-seat saloon at the other, with a lavatory, kitchen and brake compartment in the centre of the vehicle. It also had a driver's compartment at each end, so it was a very versatile carriage, and could be propelled, as seen here. When this picture was taken at Basingstoke in 1966 it seems likely that No.70155 was being shunted around the station area - hence the presence of a tail lamp. Towards the end of its career No.70155 was repainted, rather incongruously, in rail blue livery with full yellow ends, which were mandatory at the time, and it became one of the very few Maunsell coaches to receive blue livery. Withdrawal came in October 1988 and the coach was subsequently sold to the Kent & East Sussex Railway.

Colour-Rail

Royal Mail Van No.S4950S

Originating Company:	SECR	Type of Coach:	Royal Mail Sorting Van
SR Diagram No:	1204	Build Date:	1906
Length:	50ft 1in	Seating Capacity:	

This Royal Mail sorting van was one of two constructed in 1906 and it is seen here right at the end of its career at Eardley Road sidings on 18 April 1960, just a few weeks prior to withdrawal on 4 June. It is likely that it was already out of traffic when this picture was taken. The van was originally numbered 131 and had body framing of teak with mahogany panels and mouldings and was gas lit when built. It had two double doors on one side and two sliding doors (as seen here) with 3ft. openings on the other side. The underframe was of oak with iron bolsters. The bodysides were emblazoned with the words 'Royal Mail Malle Royale' in large capital letters, so passengers were left in no doubt regarding the purpose of the vehicle! In April 1907 the SECR completed two stowage vans to accompany the sorting vans. No.4950 spent almost its entire career on the London Bridge to Dover postal workings, apart from the Second World War when such trains were suspended and it was mothballed at Epsom Downs station.

R.C. Riley

Royal Mail Van No.S4950S

Mail bags were still piled high on the platform when this shot was taken at London Bridge on 22 January 1960, so presumably the departure of the 11.50pm mail train to Dover was not imminent. The vehicle nearest to the camera is a SECR specimen (as previously mentioned) while the other coach is a Southern Railway designed vehicle. Regrettably, mail trains, which were once a familiar sight throughout Great Britain, have largely disappeared.

R.C. Riley

Buffet Car No.182 formerly Pullman Car *Madeline*

Originating Company:	Pullman Car Co.	**Type of Coach:**	Pullman Buffet Car
SR Diagram No:	599	**Build Date:**	1926
Length:	57ft 1½in	**Seating Capacity:**	17 (unclassed)

This coach was one of six vehicles built by the Metropolitan Carriage, Wagon & Finance Co. in 1926 for use on the London to Tonbridge and Hastings service and was constructed with a narrow body due to the restricted width of some tunnels on that route. In 1946 it was rebuilt as a non-supplement buffet car and in the process lost its special Pullman identity and was reclassified 'Refreshment Car'. In 1958 all six cars were repainted in green livery, without names, and advertised to the public as 'Buffet Cars' - a further downgrading! Two years later, the six cars were sold by the Pullman Car Company to BR and Car No.182 became BR No.S7875 and was allocated to the Waterloo to Southampton Docks ocean liner boat trains. It is seen at an unknown location, probably Gipsy Hill, apparently forming part of an enthusiasts' special (note the paper identification on the roof boards) and was photographed on 18 October 1959. No.S7875 was withdrawn from BR service on 28 December 1963 and subsequently scrapped, but two sister vehicles, *Theodora* and *Barbara* are preserved on the Kent & East Sussex Railway.

R.C. Riley

Guard's Van No.616

Originating Company:	SECR	**Type of Coach:**	Six-wheel passenger brake van
SR Diagram No:	885	**Build Date:**	1905
Length:	32ft 0in	**Seating Capacity:**	Nil

This remarkable survivor, which was photographed at Chasewater on 5 May 1968, was built by the Metropolitan Amalgamated Railway Carriage & Wagon Company in Birmingham in April 1905 and was SECR No.719. It was renumbered 616 in the Southern Railway series and later entered departmental service as No.1601S, being used as an air raid precaution cleansing van at Bricklayers Arms. It was withdrawn in July 1946 but found further employment on the Derwent Valley Light Railway in Yorkshire and is thought to have remained in use until 1959.

David Wigley

Guard's Van No.DS1510

Originating Company:	SER	**Type of Coach:**	Six-wheel passenger brake van
SR Diagram No:	884	**Build Date:**	1899
Length:	32ft 0in	**Seating Capacity:**	Nil

This interesting van was photographed in a siding at Groombridge on 29 October 1961. It was built as South Eastern Railway No.334 by the Ashbury Railway Carriage & Wagon Company, Manchester, and was renumbered 529 at the Grouping. In its heyday this type of vehicle could be observed in the formation of Continental boat expresses. This particular specimen was withdrawn from ordinary service in November 1939 and entered departmental stock as an air raid precautions cleansing van and was later apparently employed variously as an engineer's mess van and a mobile kitchen. It lasted in this guise for seven years before being withdrawn once again. It then began yet another phase in its career in use as a static stores van at Groombridge during which time its grey livery faded to such a degree it resembled a rather ghostly white. Note the Bulleid coach just creeping into the picture on the right.

John Langford

And Finally...

One foot in the grave. The interesting selection of rolling stock stabled in Micheldever yard made it a high point (at least for enthusiasts!) of a journey down the Bournemouth line. During the era covered by this album the sidings were generally used as a dumping ground for condemned stock *en route* to the scrap merchants, so the yard presented an ever-changing scene. On 25 July 1971 the occupants included three former service vehicles which are (from left to right) Nos.DS70134, 081642, an internal use vehicle, and DS70109. These coaches were formerly Nos.1020, 7400 and 7798, which in happier times were respectively, a third class carriage, a first class vehicle and a nondescript saloon. All three coaches were later purchased by the Kent & East Sussex Railway but were eventually broken up. A withdrawn '4-Sub' unit just creeps into the shot whilst on the extreme left a '2-Bil' can just be discerned.

David Wigley